Prai
A Sudd

"How do we awaken to the transforming glory of God that is all about us? Heavenly seraphim proclaim that the earth is full of His glory—but why do we miss it? More important, how do we awaken to Jesus, who 'is the radiance of the glory of God'? In *A Sudden Glory*, Sharon Jaynes lifts the veil—and invites us right into His heart, where He speaks to our persistent ache for something more."

—ANN VOSKAMP, author of *One Thousand Gifts*

"In *A Sudden Glory*, Sharon Jaynes reminds us that the 'ache for meaning beyond the dailyness of life' is only found by embracing God's passionate desire for intimacy. This book is a treasure!"

—CAROL KENT, speaker and author of *Between a Rock and a Grace Place*

"There's no doubt about it; Sharon Jaynes's latest project is a *love story*. It's about a glorious Prince named Jesus, who is passionately wooing a world full of Cinderellas. The only problem is so many of these would-be princesses have amnesia and have forgotten the sacred romance they've been supernaturally written into. *A Sudden Glory* set off an alarm in my sleepy heart and reminded me to run toward the intimate embrace of our Redeemer!"

—LISA HARPER, Bible teacher, Women of Faith speaker, and author of *A Perfect Mess*

"*Cease striving.* Such refreshing words in a culture that seems to breed the philosophy that the more you do, the more you get. Sharon Jaynes reminds us that our spiritual yearning for more is not satisfied by checking off a to-do list of religious accomplishments. She brings us to a fresh and freeing understanding that 'in Him we live and move and have our being.' The beautiful message of *A Sudden Glory* continually reminds us of the great love our Father has lavished upon us as His children and the joy of abiding in His presence."

—KAROL LADD, author of *The Power of a Positive Woman*

"If you ache for something more, something deeper, something greater, something glorious in life and in your walk with God, Sharon Jaynes pulls back the curtain on the heart of God and all He has awaiting you! Don't settle for the mundane—live glorious! Thanks, Sharon, for helping us travel away from the ordinary, everyday, commonplace, humdrum, dull routine into God's great, grand, and glorious expedition!"

—PAM FARREL, speaker and author of *10 Secrets to Living Smart, Savvy, and Strong*

A
SUDDEN
GLORY

A SUDDEN GLORY

God's Lavish Response
to Your Ache *for* Something More

SHARON JAYNES

Best-selling author of *The Power of a Woman's Words*

MULTNOMAH
BOOKS

A SUDDEN GLORY
PUBLISHED BY MULTNOMAH BOOKS
12265 Oracle Boulevard, Suite 200
Colorado Springs, Colorado 80921

All Scripture quotations, unless otherwise indicated, are taken from the Holy Bible, New International Version®. NIV®. Copyright © 1973, 1978, 1984 by Biblica Inc.™ Used by permission of Zondervan. All rights reserved worldwide. www.zondervan.com. Scripture quotations marked (ESV) are taken from The Holy Bible, English Standard Version, copyright © 2001 by Crossway Bibles, a division of Good News Publishers. Used by permission. All rights reserved. Scripture quotations marked (KJV) are taken from the King James Version. Scripture quotations marked (MSG) are taken from The Message by Eugene H. Peterson. Copyright © 1993, 1994, 1995, 1996, 2000, 2001, 2002. Used by permission of NavPress Publishing Group. All rights reserved. Scripture quotations marked (NASB) are taken from the New American Standard Bible®. © Copyright The Lockman Foundation 1960, 1962, 1963, 1968, 1971, 1972, 1973, 1975, 1977, 1995. Used by permission. (www.Lockman.org). Scripture quotations marked (NKJV) are taken from the New King James Version®. Copyright © 1982 by Thomas Nelson Inc. Used by permission. All rights reserved. Scripture quotations marked (NLT) are taken from the Holy Bible, New Living Translation, copyright © 1996, 2004, 2007. Used by permission of Tyndale House Publishers Inc., Carol Stream, Illinois 60188. All rights reserved. Scripture quotations marked (TLB) are taken from The Living Bible, copyright © 1971. Used by permission of Tyndale House Publishers Inc., Wheaton, Illinois 60189. All rights reserved. Quotation on page 83 is NIV © 2011.

Italics in Scripture quotations reflect the author's added emphasis.

Details in some anecdotes and stories have been changed to protect the identities of the persons involved.

Grateful acknowledgment is made for the use of "Shout to the Lord," by Darlene Zschech, © 1993 Hillsong Publishing (APRA) (adm. in the US and Canada at EMICMGPublishing.com). All rights reserved. Used by permission.

ISBN 978-1-60142-408-2
ISBN 978-1-60142-409-9 (electronic)

Cover design: Kelly L. Howard

Published in the United States by WaterBrook Multnomah, an imprint of the Crown Publishing Group, a division of Random House Inc., New York.

MULTNOMAH and its mountain colophon are registered trademarks of Random House Inc.

Library of Congress Cataloging-in-Publication Data
Jaynes, Sharon.
    A sudden glory : God's lavish response to your ache for something more / Sharon Jaynes. — 1st ed.
        p. cm.
    Includes bibliographical references (p.   ).
    ISBN 978-1-60142-408-2 — ISBN 978-1-60142-409-9 (electronic)
    1. Christian women—Religious life. 2. Spirituality. I. Title.
BV4527.J393 2012
248.8'43—dc23

                                2012002174

Printed in the United States of America
2012—First Edition

10 9 8 7 6 5 4 3 2 1

SPECIAL SALES
Most WaterBrook Multnomah books are available at special quantity discounts when purchased in bulk by corporations, organizations, and special-interest groups. Custom imprinting or excerpting can also be done to fit special needs. For information, please e-mail SpecialMarkets@ WaterBrookMultnomah.com or call 1-800-603-7051.

Dedicated to Pat Edmondson

*Your joy in the Lord and love of life
have helped train my eyes and tune my ears
to discover moments of Sudden Glory
scattered throughout the pages of my days.*

CONTENTS

THE GLORY ACHE

O God, I have tasted Thy goodness, and it
has both satisfied me and made me thirsty
for more. I am painfully conscious of my
need for further grace.
—A. W. TOZER, *The Pursuit of God*

*I*t happened again.

I was not surprised.

Her words of frustration and longing spilled from her heart to my
e-mail inbox.

Dear Sharon:

I have lived a very blessed life. I have been married to the
same man for forty years. I have four beautiful daughters, who
seem to have married the perfect mates, and nine wonderful grandchildren. I was raised in a Christian home, and my

mother is still alive and healthy at eighty-five years old. My husband is retired, and we are living comfortably. I have never been abused or mistreated. I have friends, and most would say that I am a happy person. And yet, something is missing. With all the good things in my life, all I really want is a close relationship with Jesus.

I am trying, I really am. Even though I was raised in church, I married a Jewish man and drifted away from God. I gave my life to Christ at a women's Christian meeting fifteen years ago and have been pursuing God ever since. I felt that recommitment was necessary for me. It was a new beginning. Now I do an online Bible study, am an active member of a local church, visit a shut-in once a month, and help with vacation Bible school. I have taught Sunday school, and I attend church regularly and pray daily.

I have been reading and studying the Bible and know that when you seek forgiveness, it is given. I have asked God to forgive me of the choices I have made and believe that He has. Now I am asking God to let me know what His purpose is for my life. What does He want from me? What does He have planned for me? I am trying very hard to listen for His direction. I am willing to follow His path, whenever I realize what that is.

Here's the crux of my problem. After I gave my life to Christ, I joined a church and began reading the Bible daily. Yet I never experienced that overwhelming feeling of change that so many others experience. In my quiet times, when I seek to know Him better and wait quietly for answers, I do not get the nudges that others talk about. I know that some people hit rock bottom and then experience a dramatic life change accompanied by an emotional high. I sometimes wonder if I will have to experience some great trial in order to have the wonderful feelings of a true relationship with Christ.

I have worked on identifying my sins, thinking that this might help me feel closer to God. I am working on not gossiping and not being prideful or vain. I am always working on my patience. I don't have any serious vices, but I am constantly working on self-improvement. I try to start each day with quiet time, Scripture reading, and prayer. I try to have a God-focused day.

Is something wrong with me? Do other women feel this emptiness too? Should I be feeling something more? What more should I be doing? I know Christ loves me, but something is missing and I don't even know what it is. What should I do?

—Stephanie

Oh, Stephanie, I whispered, *no you are not alone. Your words echo the longings of women all around the world, and I dare say, through the ages. Why is feeling close to God so hard? Why does this faith journey seem so difficult?*

THERE MUST BE SOMETHING MORE

This was the first time I had heard from Stephanie but not the first time I had heard the heart-cry. The particulars of her story were different, but I had heard the same longing from countless others.

Most of us come to Christ with a certain "inloveness"—a stirring of emotion mixed with an inexplicable knowing that we've discovered our reason for being. But some years into our spiritual journey, the wonder that swelled during the early years ebbs into routine religion laced with busyness. And we secretly question the point of it all. *There has to be more than this,* we muse. *There has to be something more. What am I missing? What's wrong with me? I'm doing all the right things, but God seems so far away. I'm trying as hard as I can, but it never seems to be enough. What does God really want from me anyway?*

For decades, as I have had the privilege of ministering to women, I have heard the same heart-cry from those who desire to have a deep, intimate, exuberant relationship with Christ but don't know how to find it.

Perhaps you can relate. You long to feel close to God but sense there's just something lacking, that you've missed the mysterious formula to make it happen. I call this a "glory ache"—a persistent longing to experience God's presence on a daily basis. Perhaps like most women, you've tried desperately to balance the montage of mundane demands and somehow slip God into the white spaces that are few and far between. You long to spend time in the sacred with God but find the desire crowded out by the responsibilities of the secular—the daily demands that lay claim to your attention. You yearn to experience God's presence but feel far away from Him as you reach to click off the bedside lamp and collapse exhausted once again. *Maybe tomorrow,* you sigh.

Sound familiar? If so, you are not alone.

The travesty is that we allow the busyness of life to crowd out the Source of life. As the psalmist wrote, "We are merely moving shadows, and all our busy rushing ends in nothing" (Psalm 39:6, *pre-reading books*

NLT). Ann Voskamp echoes that lament: "In a world addicted to speed, I blur the moments into one unholy smear."[1]

And in that unholy smear, that blur of the world passing quickly by, we know something's not quite right. So we strike out to make it all better. And most of us are quick to think "something more" means "doing more." We ramp it up and gun the engines—sign up for a new committee, volunteer for a new cause, bake one more casserole to feed the sick. We attempt to silence the hunger pains of the heart by feeding it the bread and water of duty. And at the end of the day, while we might feel a self-induced sense of well-being, the hollowness in our souls that can only be satisfied with God echoes with the grumblings of hunger still.

We long for a sense of closeness with God, but we have a hard time putting our finger on exactly what that closeness would look like. It's just something more. Something different. A flavor we have yet to taste. A country we have yet to visit. A sunset we have yet to experience. A lover we have yet to embrace. *There has to be something more, we cry!* And we are quite right. We are craving the closeness that comes with an intimate relationship with Jesus.

So we try harder. We go to Bible studies, attend church, say our prayers, and read our devotions. Check, check, check. And yet, we constantly feel that we are somehow letting God down. With the last "amen" of the day, we sigh, *What more does God want from me?*

One January morning a few years ago, I asked God that same question. I had just finished a big writing project and was ready to tackle the next big thing for God. I snuggled in my favorite den chair with a steamy cup of coffee and my well-worn Bible to spend some alone time with my heavenly Father. I read a few verses and said my prayer. Check. Check. When I started to get up, I felt God's invisible strong hand holding me back. He wasn't finished. *Be still, and know that I am God,* He seemed to say. *Cease striving.*

Suddenly I saw myself with the disciples caught on the stormy Sea of Galilee. As I pondered the past twenty-five years of my life, I saw myself reeling in the waves of ceaseless activity. A squall of busyness raging around me—and in me. Reeling from one foamy crest of work and deadlines to the next and hanging on for dear life. In my mind's eye, the fellow passengers were not the motley crew of first-century disciples but women from every walk, trying to steady themselves in the turbulent waters of life.

"Teacher, don't you care if we drown?" they asked. "Help us!"

Then I sensed Jesus speaking to me just as He had spoken to the raucous wind and waves: *"Quiet! Be still! Settle down!"*

So I sat.

After a few moments, I realized I didn't really know how to *be quiet and settle down.* I had never mastered the full idea of "be still and know." I knew that God was God. It was the "be still" part that stumped me. Sitting still was not in my nature, and perhaps it was my nature that God was trying to tame. My "nature," or natural bent of working for God, was standing in the way of my worship of and communion with God. My daily routine of sanctioned quiet times was getting in the way of the divine romance in which He wanted me to engage.

Does it surprise you that I could say such words? Oh, friend, I am nothing if I am not honest. I have that glory ache just like you. Sometimes I can get so busy doing, doing, doing that God's gentle whisper drawing me closer is drowned out by the noises of my own making. How sad to admit that, sometimes when God extends his hand to invite me onto the dance floor of life, my dance card is already full. Many nights *I* lean over to turn out the bedside lamp, collapse in exhaustion, and sigh, *"Maybe tomorrow, Lord."*

I don't think "be still and know" comes naturally to any of us. Aren't we taught to get moving? "Keep your eye on the ball." "Focus on the target." "If you don't know where you are going, you probably won't get there." Motivational phrases for sure. But this was God talking, and He had a different message. While the world prods, "Don't just stand there; do something!" God was telling me quite the opposite: "Don't just do something; stand there."

Now He had my attention. So I stayed put.

"Okay, God," I asked, "what do You really want from me?"

He surprised me. He often does, when I take the time to listen. Acts 17:28 came to mind. I believe He put it there. "In him we live and move and have our being." *Learn what that means,* He seemed to say. I opened my Bible again and read the words, pondering each phrase individually.

In Him.

We live.

And move.

And have our being.

I sensed God speaking to my heart. *That's where you will find the secret to satisfy that glory ache. That's the answer you are searching for. That's where you will find what your sisters hunger for. You've been asking the wrong question. It's not what I want from you. It's what I want for you. And in this one little verse, you'll find the key—not just for yourself but also for others in the boat with you. This will calm the squall of your frantic heart.*

God startled me that morning. I was expecting Him to give me a new assignment—something to do for Him. Another project to complete. Another study to devour. Another cause to support. But He surprised me. It was none of the above. It was one verse: "In him we live and move and have our being."

I wondered, *Could this be the key to unlock the door behind which the salve to satisfy that glory ache was hidden? The door upon which I had been knocking far too long?* I was excited to accept God's invitation as He extended His hand for mine.

ASKING THE WRONG QUESTION

Could it be that we have made our relationship with God far too difficult? We strive so hard to draw closer to the heart of God. And all the while, God's outstretched hand is reaching to draw us in. Another translation of Psalm 46:10 reads, "Cease striving and know that I am God" (NASB). *Cease striving.*

For over half a century, I had been striving, pursuing, and seeking God. And like a cat chasing its tail, I had been going in circles. Circling in the wilderness with the Israelites, if you will. Saved from slavery, for sure. Headed to my own personal Promised Land, hopefully. But somehow stuck in the wilderness, wandering, ever circling but not quite reaching Jordan's shore.

And I am not alone. Statistics show that one of the top desires of Christians is to grow closer to God.[2] During a recent poll, 65 percent of churchgoers said they were declining or on a plateau in their spiritual growth.[3] On the other hand, Peter wrote: "His divine power has given us everything we need for life and godliness through our knowledge of him who called us by his own glory and goodness" (2 Peter 1:3). We have everything we need to experience the ever-growing, continually maturing, abundant life. So why aren't we? Why are most of us languishing on the desert plateaus of mediocrity and complacency? Why are most of us satisfied munching on the predigested truths of teachers rather than pulling up to the banquet table and feasting with God at a table set for two?

"God, what do you really want from me?"

I've pondered that question since the genesis of my relationship with Christ. Perhaps you have too. When you boil down all the water from the diluted soup of questions men and women have simmered in their hearts through the centuries, this is the one question left in the pot. And somehow we feel that if we could answer that one question, we would discover why that glory ache persists and how to satisfy our yearning.

I had asked the question a thousand times, but on that one frosty January morning, I got quiet enough to listen. And then, in the stillness, He showed me that I and my busy sisters have been asking the wrong question.

Rather than ask God what He wants *from* us, we need to ask Him what He wants *for* us.

I meditated on Acts 17:28 throughout the following year, after the day God whetted my appetite with the possibilities wrapped up in those ten little words. I came to realize that what He wants *for* us is to sense His presence, experience His love, and delight in intimate relationship as we *live and move and have our being* in sacred union with Him. And when we do, He opens our eyes to His glory all around and the ache for something more is soothed.

Glory Defined

Have you ever wondered why you were created? You were created for God's glory and to glorify God (Isaiah 43:7), because it pleased Him to do so (Ephesians 1:5). The concept of glory can be a difficult idea to wrap our human minds around. It seems so otherworldly. We can catch glimpses of its meaning throughout Scripture, but then like a shooting star that appears for just a moment, it quickly slips away into the vast expanse of God's infinite wisdom. But let's see what we can know about this bigger-than-life word.

In the Old Testament, the most common Hebrew word for "glory" is *kābôd,* meaning "weight, honor, or esteem." The Bible associates God's glory with how He manifests Himself or makes His presence known. Some theologians refer to these as theophanies. He made His presence known in a consuming fire (Exodus 24:16–17), a moving cloud (Exodus 13:21), and a still small voice (1 Kings 19:12). His glory is reflected in creation (Psalm 19:1) and in His sovereign control of history (Acts 17:26). His glory is made known through the life of simple human beings like you and me.

The same concept of God's glory is in the New Testament in the Greek word *doxa,* which means "glory, honor, and splendor." John wrote, "The Word became flesh and made his dwelling among us. We have seen his *glory,* the *glory* of the One and Only, who came from the Father, full of grace and truth" (John 1:14). After Jesus's first miracle, turning the water into wine, John wrote: "This, the first of his miraculous signs, Jesus performed at Cana in Galilee. He thus revealed his *glory,* and his disciples put their faith in him" (John 2:11). In Hebrews 1:3, the writer reveals this about Jesus: "The Son is the radiance of God's *glory* and the exact representation of his being, sustaining all things by his powerful word."

The verb form, "to glorify," is *doxazo,* and primarily means "to magnify, extol, praise, to ascribe honor to God, acknowledging Him as to His being, attributes and acts,"[4] i.e., His glory. It is the revelation and manifestation of all that He has and is. When we glorify God, we are giving a display or manifestation—or a reflection—of His character. To magnify God is to make Him easy to see. Jesus said that the disciples would *glorify* God when they bore fruit (John 15:8). Through their actions, they would point others to God and make Him easy to see.

God's glory is how He makes Himself known. It is almost incomprehensible to think that He would choose mere human beings to accomplish such a task. But as Scripture tells us, we were created in His image (Genesis 1:26) and as a display of His glory (Isaiah 43:7). You were created to make God recognizable to others—to show others what God is like. He makes Himself recognizable to us and through us. The *glory* of any created thing is when it is fully fulfilling the purpose for which it was created...and that includes you and me.

Glory is a big word—a weighty word. In this book we are going to zoom in on one aspect of glory—how God makes Himself known in your life as you *live and move and have your being in Him.*

Can you remember a time when you sensed God's presence and you were absolutely sure it was Him? Perhaps it was when you first believed, or maybe it happened just yesterday. You may have felt an overwhelming sense of His love, received an answer to prayer, felt an inexplicable peace, or witnessed a miracle. But when it happened—oh, when it happened—you knew you had encountered the Divine. The moment came and went, and you were awestruck. Do you remember it? I call those moments when God makes Himself known to you personally *a sudden glory*—an intimate moment with your Creator, the Lover of your soul, a glimpse of heaven.

To illustrate what I mean by this, consider how Sheldon Vanauken, author of *A Severe Mercy,* describes the moment he knew he was in love with his wife, Davy:

> One who has never been in love might mistake either infatuation or a mixture of affection and sexual attraction for being in love. But when the "real thing" happens, there is no doubt. A man in the jungle at night, as someone said, may suppose a hyena's growl to be a lion's; but when he hears the lion's growl, he knows [full] well it's a lion. So with the genuine inloveness. So with Davy and me. A sudden glory.[5]

I have been in the jungle and heard the lion's roar. I knew full well it was Him. So with the genuine inloveness. So with Jesus and me. A sudden glory. Time and time again.

All throughout our lives, I dare say, throughout our days, we will experience a sudden glory in unpredictable moments. Or, at least we could.

A friend shared a moment of sudden glory in her life:

> Life was hard after my divorce. With no child support and only a part-time job for income, there were days when I didn't know how I would put dinner on the table for myself and my four children. I often had to choose between buying groceries or paying the electric bill. On one such day, I walked to the mailbox praying

I wouldn't find another cut-off notice from the utility company. Thankfully there was nothing of the sort. Instead I found an envelope that had no return address, and inside it was a note that read, "Jesus loves you." Tucked behind the note was a grocery store gift card for an amount that would buy groceries for at least a week.

In that moment I felt as if God had wrapped His arms around me and whispered to my heart, "I see you. I love you. I care." His presence was suddenly so real that all I could do was stand there and cry.

These moments are the salve for the glory ache. They are the manna moments to stay the hunger until we finally reach heaven's home. Do you yearn for those glory moments? Well, guess what. God longs to give them to you even more than you yearn for them!

THE CALLING OUT OF GOD

Eden was full of God's glory—breathtaking beauty with unbroken union and constant communion with God. But as we know, something went terribly wrong, and Adam and Eve found themselves naked and ashamed. And what was the first thing they did when that happened?

They hid.

They hid from God.

"Then the man and his wife heard the sound of the LORD God as he was walking in the garden in the cool of the day, and they hid from the LORD God among the trees of the garden. But the LORD God called to the man, 'Where are you?'" (Genesis 3:8–9). God called out.

Be still. There is a healer...

God.

Called.

Out.

"Where are you?" God asked. It was the very first question in the Bible, and it was asked by an all-knowing God. He still asks that very question today. Perhaps you've heard it as well. I have.

The real tragedy of Adam and Eve's disobedience was that union between God and mankind was broken. Shattered. Destroyed. But as soon as Eve sank her teeth into the forbidden fruit, the shadow of the cross rose on the horizon and God's redemptive plan to restore all that we had lost was set in motion. All through the rest of the Old Testament, from Genesis 3:9 to Malachi 4:6, we read of God calling humanity back to Himself.

We read of cycles of humanity's fellowship with God, followed by humanity's rebellion against God, followed by God's wooing humanity back in the midst of difficult circumstances, followed by humanity's repentance, followed by humanity's fellowship with God, followed by humanity's rebellion against God, followed by God's wooing humanity back in the midst of difficult circumstances, followed by humanity's repentance, followed by humanity's fellowship with God, followed by…

And all along God continues His passionate pursuit of the human heart as He relentlessly romances us, His image bearers, and calls out to us first one way, then another.

Interestingly, the Hebrew word for "Scripture" is *mikra*, which means "the calling out of God."[6] And isn't that what the Bible really is? The calling out of God to draw mankind back to Himself? To restore our original glory through the finished work of Jesus Christ? He begins with *calling out* that very first question: "Where are you?" He ends it the same. "I stand at the door and knock" (Revelation 3:20).

The Bible tells us, "All have sinned and fall short of the glory of God" (Romans 3:23). There is not one of us who is completely and perfectly living the life that God had intended in the garden. But the good news is that Christ in us is the hope of glory (Colossians 1:27). It is through union with Jesus that glory moments occur. Without Christ in us, we are not even able to detect or reflect God's glory at all. And yet, that was God's original intent for us "in the beginning."

Most people would agree that we are born with an inherent inner nagging that there has to be something more than what we see. Solomon wrote: "He has also *set eternity in the hearts* of men" (Ecclesiastes 3:11). No matter how humanity has tried to satisfy the hunger, quench the thirst, or mask the reality of God's existence, eternity continues pulling at the heart. A longing to experience God persists. The glory ache is a chronic throb.

But here is the good news! Aren't you ready for some good news? This is not our final home! We are merely passing through this thing called life. And until those who know Christ leave this earth and enter God's glory once and for all, until we inhale eternity, He gives us *glimpses of glory* right here on earth! Moments of sudden glory abound, if we will but take the time to recognize them, to embrace them, to enjoy them…to taste and see that the Lord is good!

And how do we do that? It is all wrapped up in that little verse that God filled my mind with on that chilly January morning: "In him we live and move and have our being" (Acts 17:28).

The Road to Glory Moments

For twelve months I pondered the words *in Him we live and move and have our being* before I put pen to paper. I listened to others traveling down the road with me. Women trying to juggle taking care of children, aging parents, longing husbands, demanding work schedules, unending household chores, and faltering faith. Women trying to fit God into their busy schedules and never feeling like they do it well. I've seen guilt become a constant companion as women crouch behind the bushes with Adam and Eve rather than walk with God unashamed.

Do you long to recapture the radiant wonder of your early years of faith? Have you felt the hunger in your own heart for something more? Have you experienced the nagging ache to catch glimpses of God's glory here on earth?

For me, that early wonder was energized by the emotional surges of a teenager falling in love with Jesus for the very first time. Passion comes easy during those years when youths dive into the sea of new discoveries with reckless abandon. But as we surface to breathe in the air of adulthood, we tend to float along on the current of Christianity and swim in the school of other like-minded saints. That's not a bad place to be. It is safe. But it is the bold and the brave who venture from the saintly swarm, venture into the deep sea of grace, and explore the depths of God's fathomless wonder. Treasures in the deep are waiting to be discovered by those willing to leave the surface and plunge headlong into God's all-encompassing presence.

I want to experience God anew, not just today but every day. I don't want a tent revival religion that stokes the embers into a bonfire for a few days or even a few weeks. But I want to experience God's presence with every breath. Is that your desire as well? I believe the map to such an existence is tucked inside that one little verse…*in Him we live and move and have our being.*

C. S. Lewis quoted historic author Dr. Samuel Johnson in *Mere Christianity,* "People need to be reminded more often than they need to be instructed."[7] Throughout the pages of this book, I hope you will be reminded of God's passionate pursuit of your heart and let yourself be caught all over again. I pray that you will be reawakened to the deep desire to know Him intimately. For some, an intimate relationship with Jesus may be a new idea altogether; for others, a reawakening of a forgotten or waning romance.

I find myself kneeling with Tozer and echoing his poignant words:

O God, the Triune God, I want to want Thee; I long to be filled with longing; I thirst to be made more thirsty still. Show me Thy glory, I pray Thee, so that I may know Thee indeed. Begin in mercy a new work of love within me. Say to my soul, "Rise up my love, my fair one, and come away." Then give me grace to rise and follow Thee up from this misty lowland where I have wandered so long.[8]

Peer with me through the lattice as the Lover of your soul comes running.

Listen! My lover!
    Look! Here he comes,
leaping across the mountains,
    bounding over the hills.

My lover is like a gazelle or a young stag.

Look! There he stands behind our wall,
gazing through the windows,

peering through the lattice.

My lover spoke and said to me,

"Arise, my darling,

my beautiful one, and come with me.

See! The winter is past;

the rains are over and gone.

Flowers appear on the earth;

the season of singing has come.

the cooing of doves

is heard in our land.

The fig tree forms its early fruit;

the blossoming vines spread their fragrance.

Arise, come, my darling;

my beautiful one, come with me."

(Song of Songs 2:8–13)

As you turn the following pages, I pray that you'll begin to see new patterns of truth emerge—as if peering through a kaleidoscope at God's love. And my prayer is that you will begin to grasp the truth of how God really feels about you and what He really wants, not just *from* you but, more importantly, *for* you. My prayer is that you will begin to see many displays of sudden glory throughout the moments of your days so that you will have an undeniable assurance of His presence and love as you *live and move and have your being in Him.*

RECOGNIZING GOD'S
PASSIONATE PURSUIT

> So long as we imagine it is we who have to
> look for God, we must often lose heart. But it
> is the other way about: He is looking for us.
> —SIMON TUGWELL, *Prayer: Living with God*

I was in college when I first eyed my husband. He was sitting on
the floor at a friend's Bible study gathering with his back against
the wall, dressed in scruffy jeans and a red flannel shirt with the sleeves
rolled halfway up his muscular forearms. His thick brown hair and
chocolate-brown eyes left me weak in the knees. And the best part was
that this handsome hunk of a man had a tattered Bible in his lap. He
laughed easily, prayed humbly, and read intently. I was smitten from
the first time I laid eyes on Steve.

After a few weeks, he finally asked me out on a date. We continued seeing each other over the next several weeks, but I was still accepting invitations from others as well. One night, Steve asked me to a college football game, and I agreed to go. Then he said, "Can I just ask you? Will you go with me to all of the football games for the rest of the year?"

"I'm not going to answer that question," I replied. "You'll just have to ask me each week."

Looking back on those early days, what I was really saying was that I wanted to be pursued. None of this blanket-invitation-for-the-entire-fall business. I wanted to be wooed and won. Even though he had me the moment I saw him sitting on the shag carpet floor, I didn't want *him* to know that. I wanted him to show me I was worth putting forth the effort to capture my heart. Isn't that the desire of every woman's heart?

And nobody does it better than God.

GOD'S GRAND PURSUIT

The entire Bible from Genesis 3 to Revelation 22:21 is a record of God's passionate pursuit of the human heart: Noah, Abraham, Isaac, Jacob, Joseph, Moses, Joshua, Samuel, a string of kings, both good and bad, intermingled with prophets wooing and warning God's people. We end the last chapter of the Old Testament with silence. And then four hundred years later, God breaks the holy hush with the cry of a babe in a manger as the story picks back up in Bethlehem.

From God's first question, "Where are you?" until Jesus's final words on the cross, "It is finished," we see God drawing mankind with *cords of kindness* that sometimes appear anything but kind—drawing people back to Himself with *ties of love* (see Hosea 11:4). We've wiggled and wrangled trying to break free of those cords, but He continues to lasso us with love and draw us in again.

Passionate pursuit. He's pulled out all the stops. Moved heaven and earth—literally—to win us back, to reestablish the glory that was lost in the garden. As Tozer said, "The whole work of God in redemption is to undo the tragic effects of that foul revolt, and to bring us back again into right and eternal relationship with Himself."[9]

Most of us feel that we have to pursue God continually, as if He were hard to find. And as long as we believe that, our faith journey *will* be difficult. It will be arduous. But didn't Jesus say, "Come to me, all you who are weary and burdened, and I will give you *rest*. Take my yoke upon you and learn from me, for I am gentle and humble in heart, and you will find *rest* for your souls. For my yoke is easy and my burden is light" (Matthew 11:28–30)? And yet, *easy* and *light* are not words that come quickly to mind when women explain their faith journey to me.

Make no mistake about it. God always makes the first move. Where do you think this glory ache comes from? God put it there! He is wooing you, stirring you, awakening a longing for Him in your soul. Jesus said, "No one can come to me unless the Father who sent me draws him" (John 6:44). He tunes the violin and pulls the bow across the strings of your heart and waits for you to recognize the melody wooing you into relationship with Him.

God has had His eye on you since before the foundation of the earth. The Message says it this way: "Long before he laid down earth's foundations, he had us in mind, had settled on us as the focus of his love, to be made whole and holy by his love" (Ephesians 1:4, MSG). My heart resonates with the words of Simon Tugwell: "So long as we imagine it is we who have to look for God, we must often lose heart. But it is the other way about—He is looking for us."[10]

When you come to Christ, the Bible says that your dead spirit comes to life! We often refer to this as being born again, the phrase Jesus used when He explained new birth to Nicodemus (John 3:7). You are now complete in Christ with a living body, soul, *and* spirit. It is a glory moment of the best kind. However, this is not the last of those moments. It is only the first. God does not end His pursuit with your profession of faith, but He continues a day-by-day, moment-by-moment display of His presence as you *live and move and have your being in Him.* And those who recognize His grand (and sometimes subtle) displays experience moments of sudden glory.

But all too often we stop short. We walk the aisle or raise a hand. We confess Jesus as Savior but stop short of the glory life God has planned all along. He continues His pursuit in order to draw you into a deeper, more intimate relationship with Him. He longs to tell you His secrets—to "confide" in you (Psalm 25:14). Moments of sudden glory are waiting to be experienced, if you will but recognize His extended hand and grab hold.

As I mentioned before, I have been in an all-out pursuit of God for most of my adult life. But I had been looking through the wrong end of the telescope. When He turned it around, the truth became clear. I was much too large and God far too small. I began to see that He was the one pursuing me. He was the one with outstretched hands inviting me to *live and move and have my being in Him.*

It feels almost sacrilegious to think of God pursuing me. He is God. I am but dust. And yet God does pursue *me.* He does pursue *you.* I am undone trying to grasp an inkling of understanding, the incomprehensible possibility and the absurdity of it all. Shouldn't I be the one pursuing God? Isn't that what I've done all my life? Isn't that what theologians wrote about for centuries? And yet, everywhere I look, I catch glimpses of God pursuing me—romancing me.

I warm at Sheldon Vanauken's musings of the time he was just getting to know the woman who stole his heart.

Her eyes, I had not failed to observe, were indeed beautiful: long eyes, grey eyes with a hint of sea-green in certain lights. A wide brow and a small determined chin—a heart-shaped face. Rather suddenly, without previous reflection on the matter, it began to appear to me that heart-shaped faces were perhaps the best kind. She was not very tall, and I was; but now I wondered whether, after all, small girls were not more—well, more adorable, sort of. Especially when they had shining brown hair and low lovely voices and beauteous eyes.

We talked and looked at each other by firelight, for I had switched out the lamps. She told me about a coasting voyage she had taken all by herself, just because she wanted to be on a ship and the sea.... There had been a storm, and the passengers had run or been shoo'd below; but Jean [Davy] had crept forward into the bows and crouched in a coil of line, wet and loving the spray and the plunging bow. This story appealed to me beyond words. Then we discovered that we both loved poetry; she capped one of my quotations. We grinned at each other, and were linked by metre.... Then she said something about how beauty hurts. "What! You too?" I exclaimed, in effect. "You know *that*? The pain of beauty? I thought I was the only one."[11]

I envision Vanauken captivated by Davy and her storytelling—hanging on every word she said, yet distracted by her beauty at the same time. Can you see it? Oh, dear sister, that is nothing compared to how God feels about you. He's crazy about you!

In God's all-out pursuit of my heart, of your heart, He sings through a child's voice, speaks through a bird's call, shouts through the claps of thunder, and calls out through the rising sun. What is the key to experiencing God's passionate pursuit? It's simple really. We must recognize and acknowledge His presence as we *live and move and have our being in Him.* Acts 17:28 must be more than a nice Bible verse; it must become a way of life. When it does, sudden glory moments will fill our lives and take our breath away. It is a divine romance of the purest kind.

THE BEAUTY OF ROMANTIC LOVE

Aren't you glad that God refers to the Church as the bride of Christ? I asked my husband what pictures come into his mind when he reads God's description of the Church as the bride of Christ. He gave me a strange look and said, "None, really." I'll admit, I can't picture Steve walking down the aisle in a flowing wedding gown. But oh, sister, I can see myself dressed in a satin and lace, pearl-studded gown with a flowing veil and walking down the aisle of heaven to meet Jesus—my heavenly Bridegroom. Can't you? What glorious imagery God has given to His female image bearers.

Perhaps one of the most romantic books in the Bible is the Song of Songs, or as some translations title it, the Song of Solomon. While it can be read as King Solomon's wooing of the Shulammite woman working in the fields, many theologians, including Augustine, Matthew Henry, Charles Spurgeon, Hudson Taylor, and at least one gal from the South see it as an allegory of Jesus wooing the heart of His bride.

I have been like the Shulammite woman who questioned Solomon's pursuit. She felt unworthy of her suitor's advances. "Do not stare at me because I am dark, because I am darkened by the sun," she cried (Song of Songs 1:6). Her hands were stained from tending her brothers' vineyard. Her skin was burnt by the blazing sun. Her feet were callused from walking barefoot on hardened ground. But the king looked past all the outward signs of a hard-lived life and saw only her beauty.

When I first read those words through the lens of Jesus pursuing me, tears filled my eyes. And yet, the tears were not for the Shulammite woman. The tears were for myself.

I grew up in a home riddled with cyclical bursts of physical violence and constant emotional turmoil. My father drank very heavily and my parents fought, both verbally and physically, in front of me. Many nights I went to bed, pulled the covers up around my chin, and prayed that I would hurry up and go to sleep to shut out the noise of the yelling, screaming, and arguing in the next room. My parents were so wrapped up in their own problems, they were unsure how to show love to their children. I lived in a beautiful house, and all my physical needs were cared for. But my heart was hungry for something I couldn't define. An undercurrent of inferiority, insecurity, and inadequacy ran through my entire existence and became the window through which I viewed my little world.

From my earliest remembrance, I felt that I wasn't good enough, smart enough, or pretty enough. Looking back through my scrapbook of photos, I was actually a cute little girl. However, when someone *feels* ugly, the mirror on the wall somehow bypasses the reflection in the glass and goes right to the heart. *No wonder my daddy doesn't love me,* I thought on many occasions.

And yet, the King spied me in the fields and wooed me. Through a two-year courtship, Jesus pursued my adolescent heart until I finally stopped shunning His advances and allowed myself to be caught. "I am my beloved's, and his desire is for me" (Song of Solomon 7:10, ESV). Every girl's dream.

Soak in these words from the Song of Songs and read them as God's words of pursuit spoken to you.

> "I liken you, my darling, to a mare harnessed to one of the chariots of Pharaoh.... How beautiful you are, my darling! Oh, how beautiful! Your eyes are doves." (Song of Songs 1:9, 15)

> "Like a lily among thorns is my darling among the maidens.... My dove in the clefts of the rock, in the hiding places on the mountainside, show me your face, let me hear your voice; for your voice is sweet, and your face is lovely." (Song of Songs 2:2, 14)

> "How beautiful you are, my darling! Oh, how beautiful! Your eyes behind your veil are doves. Your hair is like a flock of goats descending from Mount Gilead. Your teeth are like a flock of sheep just shorn, coming up from the washing.... Your lips are like a scarlet ribbon; your mouth is lovely.... All beautiful you are, my darling; there is no flaw in you." (Song of Songs 4:1–3, 7)

More than the love story between a woman who felt unworthy of attention and a man captivated by her beauty, the Song of Songs is a beautiful picture of Jesus wooing and winning His bride…you. You have captured Jesus's attention just as surely as the Shulammite maiden captured the young king's who eyed her in the fields.

There are many different types of love: motherly love, friendship love, patriotic love, and a host of other shades and varieties. But romantic love brings with it colors and hues that are specific and unique from every other on the spectrum of emotions. Lovers are consumed with ways to make each other happy. They long for together times and feel a sense of loss when apart. Lovers are willing to sacrifice just about anything to be together. They lie awake at night dreaming up ways to make the other happy. An embrace. A kiss. A word. A look. Each of these ordinary movements between friends or acquaintances becomes rapturous between lovers. How lovely that God has chosen romantic love to describe how He feels about you. And what He really desires is for you to express that love in return in an intimate relationship.

But you must be careful, for there will always be other suitors who will attempt to lure you into their nets with false promises of a happy life.

THE LURE OF LESSER LOVERS

Yes, you are His. He is yours. So why does He continue to woo us, to romance us on a daily basis? Because our minds forget. Spiritual amnesia runs rampant as we wander off to the wooing of other lovers.

"Step right up!" the barkers of the world's Big Top circus call. "Come and see the greatest show on earth!" And even though we know in our hearts we're going to be disappointed, we enter the tent flaps, find our way to the seat marked on the ticket stub, and wait to be entertained and amazed with all the world has to offer. In the end, we are always disappointed. This was not the greatest show after all. And even though we don't deserve it, God woos us yet again.

Sometimes I fear we are like Scarlett O'Hara in *Gone with the Wind.* Throughout the entire story, Rhett Butler tried to win her heart, but Scarlett was smitten by the milquetoast Ashley Wilkes. Finally, as the story comes to a close, Rhett walks away in frustration. "I feel sorry for you, Scarlett," he declares. "You are throwing away love with both hands and grabbing for that which will never love you."

As I watched the movie, I kept thinking, *Doesn't she see how much Rhett really loves her? He'd move heaven and earth to please her, if she would but let him. Why is she going after someone who would never make her truly happy?*

And we are Scarlett, ignoring the only one who can make us truly happy and chasing after figments of our imagination…things that will never make us happy—milquetoast lovers who pale in the shadow of the Lover of our soul. Of course, in the end, Scarlett realizes her love for Rhett and runs home to tell him so. But it is too late.

As with most analogies, this one has a fatal flaw: Jesus will never throw up his hands and walk away. "Here I am!" Jesus says. "I stand at the door and knock" (Revelation 3:20).

THE GREATEST SUDDEN GLORY OF ALL

Two of my favorite words in the Bible are *but God.* For example, "Because the patriarchs were jealous of Joseph, they sold him as a slave into Egypt. *But God* was with him" (Acts 7:9).

I have many "but God" stories in my life too. I grew up with a little-girl ache to have a daddy who loved me...*but God* used a woman in my neighborhood to tell me about a heavenly Father who loved me enough to give His only Son for me. I lived in bondage to feelings of inferiority, insecurity, and inadequacy...*but God* showed me how to have unshakable confidence in Christ by knowing who I am, where I am, and what I have in Him. I felt that God didn't love me enough to answer my prayer for a second child...*but God* showed me how much He *did* love me by trusting me with spiritual children all around the world.

Perhaps you have some wonderful "but God" stories in your life as well. God's pursuit of the human heart is the greatest "but God" story of all time. At just the right time on God's kingdom calendar, the curtain rose on God's master plan for the redemption of mankind as Gabriel stepped onto the stage announcing the upcoming birth of Jesus to a young teenage girl named Mary. God sent His Son, Jesus, to pass through the birth canal of a virgin and into the world as a babe as the Word became flesh and lived among us (John 1:14).

The religious leaders of Jesus's day didn't recognize who Jesus was or what He came to do. They saw him as a threat to their pious rules and regulations. Through a series of twists and turns orchestrated by the hand of God, Jesus was crucified on a Roman cross. At first glance, it appears that angry men took Jesus's life, but the reality is that Jesus freely gave His life. Jesus gave His life as a sacrifice for our sin so that we could be reconciled or brought back into oneness with God. "*But God* demonstrates his own love for us in this: While we were still sinners, Christ died for us" (Romans 5:8).

At the very moment Jesus took His last breath, the veil in the temple's holy of holies, which kept people from entering God's presence, was torn from top to bottom, opening the way for the holy matrimony of God and mankind to be reestablished once again. Yes, God made a way, but we still have a choice whether or not to accept this wonderful gift of abundant life on earth (see John 10:10) and eternal life in heaven (see John 3:16). "If you confess with your mouth, 'Jesus is Lord,' and believe in your heart that God raised him from the dead, you will be saved" (Romans 10:9). God so loved the world...but He still leaves us with a choice.

And so God pursues you. He's pulled out all the stops to draw you into a personal relationship with Him. He is not interested in your having a religion. Oh, friend, religion will never satisfy the glory ache in your heart. It didn't satisfy the Old Testament Israelites or the New Testament Pharisees, and it won't satisfy you. He longs to be joined with you in an intimate, ongoing, personal, exuberant, exciting relationship filled with moments of sudden glory. I cannot say in just a few words all that God has done in the great pursuit of the human heart through the death and resurrection of His beloved Son. I pray that you will dig deep into the Scriptures and discover more about His amazing gift and catch a glimpse of just how much God loves you.

A sudden glory of the most glorious kind.

THE KING AND HIS MAIDEN

Soren Kierkegaard crafted a parable titled "The King and His Maiden" in order to demonstrate the lengths God went to, to win our hearts. It goes something like this:

Suppose there was a king who loved a humble maiden. The king was like no other king. Every statesman trembled before his power. No one dared breathe a word against him, for he had the strength to crush all opponents.

And yet this mighty king was melted by love for a humble maiden who lived in a poor village in his kingdom. How could he declare his love for her? In an odd sort of way, his kingliness tied his hands. If he brought her to the palace and crowned her head with jewels and clothed her body in royal robes, she would surely not resist—no one dared resist him. But would she love him?

She would say she loved him, of course, but would she truly? Or would she live with him in fear, nursing a private grief for the life she had left behind? Would she be happy at his side? How could he know for sure? If he rode to her forest cottage in his royal carriage, with an armed escort waving bright banners, that too would overwhelm her. He did not want a cringing subject. He wanted a lover, an equal. He wanted her to forget that he was a king and she a humble maiden and to let shared love cross the gulf between them. For it is only in love that the unequal can be made equal.

The king, convinced he could not elevate the maiden without crushing her freedom, resolved to descend to her. Clothed as a beggar, he approached her cottage with a worn cloak fluttering loose about him. This was not just a disguise—the king took on a totally new identity—he had renounced his throne to declare his love and to win hers.

Likewise, the King, your King, lowered Himself to a place of putting on human flesh in His pursuit of your heart. Paul described it this way:

[Jesus] who, being in very nature God,
   did not consider equality with God something to
      be grasped,
but made himself nothing,
   taking the very nature of a servant,
   being made in human likeness.
And being found in appearance as a man,
   he humbled himself
   and became obedient to death—
   even death on a cross!
Therefore God exalted him to the highest place
   and gave him the name that is above every name,
that at the name of Jesus every knee should bow,
   in heaven and on earth and under the earth,
and every tongue confess that Jesus Christ is Lord,
   to the glory of God the Father. (Philippians 2:6–11)

Why would God do such a thing? Because He loves you and longs to have an intimate, personal relationship with you. It was a high price to pay, but Jesus knew you were worth it.

Oh, friend, you are not only chosen, you are pursued to the utmost! Chosen. Pursued. Loved. And when you understand the great lengths God has gone through and continues to go through to win your love, it changes how you view life.

Lens of Love

Brenda's mother was a bitter woman. Nothing was ever good enough for her. In her eyes, her yard was never groomed well enough, her home was never clean enough, her décor was never refined enough, her husband was never affectionate enough, her jewelry never big enough, her friends never giving enough, her pastor never attentive enough, her heat never warm enough, her bank account never large enough, and so on, and so on.

All her life, Brenda had been reminded that she wasn't a good daughter. "You don't come to see me as much as you should," her mother said. "Joyce's daughter gave her a big surprise party last week." "Martha's daughter made her curtains for her kitchen." "Carol's daughter takes her out to lunch once a week." Feeling that no matter what she did it would never be enough to satisfy her mother, Brenda gave up trying and tore up the ticket for the guilt trips. She refused to ride that train ever again.

Brenda's parents had never enjoyed a good marriage, and after her father died, a new man came into her mother's life. He wooed and won her heart, and they quickly became engaged. With this new love in her life, Brenda's mother was a changed woman. The grass was greener, the sun was brighter, and suddenly Brenda was a better daughter.

"Oh, Brenda, I just love you so much," her mom gushed. "I feel like we are getting closer and closer all the time. You are becoming such a precious daughter to me."

Brenda told me about this story and laughed. "You see, Sharon," she began, "I hadn't changed at all. I still went to see her with the same frequency, called her about the same amount as I always had, and engaged in the same shallow conversation that had been the norm our entire lives. I hadn't changed a thing, but all of a sudden, I was a great daughter."

"What do you think made the difference?" I asked.

"She was in love," Brenda answered. "But probably more than that, she felt pursued and desired. Bill told her she was beautiful and doted over her like a queen. That changed her entire perspective on life."

As Solomon observed, what each of us longs for is unfailing love (see Proverbs 19:22). We dream of a love that will stay fresh and new every morning—a love that will never die. When we understand that we have that love in Jesus, it changes our perspective on life. God has pulled out all the stops. He's done more than give you the moon. He's given you His Son.

You can have a head knowledge of God, but until you embrace the truth of His passionate pursuit of your soul and taste the sweetness of His love on the palate of your heart, your life will lack a certain joy.

When you understand that you are pursued and deeply loved by God, the sun shines brighter, the leaves wave greener, the scents smell sweeter, and the future is bursting with promise. It changes everything.

A sudden glory.

THE RELENTLESS ROMANCE

Steve and I were driving home from dinner when I posed a question about romance.

"Steve, I heard someone once say that a woman defines romance as the feeling of being continually pursued. What do you think about that?"

"I don't think that is very realistic, or practical," he replied. "A man can't continually pursue a woman. Why should he? A man pursues a woman, but at some point, she has to make a decision to marry him or not. To let herself be caught or walk away. A decision has to be made. The pursing has to stop at some point."

"And I think that is one of the problems in marriages today," I answered back. "The man stops pursuing the woman's heart after she says, 'I do.'"

"I don't understand what you mean," he said. "You pursue something to catch it. When you get married, that means you caught her."

"I know it doesn't make sense to a man," I continued. "But a woman wants to continually *feel* pursued. Maybe that's why married women escape with movies like *Pride and Prejudice* or get absorbed in romance novels. They are trying to grasp for, cling to, or stir up that feeling of being pursued. But for a guy, after the ink on the marriage license dries, it seems he thinks the need for pursuit dries up as well. The bride and groom walk across the moat of singleness, into the castle of marriage, and he pulls the drawbridge up as if it's a done deal. The End."

"But a man can't spend his life pursuing someone he's already captured," Steve argued.

"Why not?" I asked.

Oh, friend, are you getting tired? I know this conversation made no sense to Steve. And listen, he is a very romantic guy. He puts forth more effort than most men I know. But this idea of romance being a continual pursuit was beyond his male ability to comprehend or execute.

Not so with God. He gets it. He does it.

C. S. Lewis argued that the most fundamental thing is not *how we think of God* but rather *how God thinks of us.* "How God thinks of us is not only more important, but infinitely more important."[12] God thinks that you are worth romancing with glory moments to capture your heart time and time again.

The question is, do we get it? Do we see God's continual wooing of our heart? Daily? Hourly? Do we recognize the romance of God in routine life?

Right smack-dab in the middle of writing this chapter, God sent me a love note. I stopped writing, turned aside, and paid attention. Then I opened my journal and jotted it down. It may seem out of place here, but I want to show you how God can interrupt and infuse your life with sudden glory moments. Some ridiculously outrageous and others relatively subtle. Here's my journal entry:

It is gray outside. The sky is gray and in turn, the lake beyond my window is gray. The water reflects the sky in a monochromatic palate of gray. The gray trees are bare with a smattering of dead, brown leaves that refuse to release their grip. A naked weeping willow's graceful gray fingers wave with a gentle breeze. And a light drizzle falls from the sky. More gray. I'm writing today. Gray words on a white screen.

And in the middle of my gray world, a vibrant red cardinal is perched on a nearby limb. His face is ringed in black. His Mohawk feathers stand perfectly groomed atop his regal head. His orange beak accents his crimson face. He looks at me and keeps me company for hours. I wonder if he even knows the joy he brings to my pale world today. I wonder if he is God's love note to me. I choose to believe so. In the grayness, God has sent me a splash of color. And I swoon.

When you expect God to make His presence known, you begin to see His hand and hear His voice in moments of sudden glory—*as you live and move and have your being in Him.* Signs of His presence brighten even the dullest days when you have eyes open to see. When you tune your senses to God's timbre, you begin to hear His song. Receptivity and attentiveness are the frequency of His voice. Hearing God's voice and sensing His presence is not difficult, but it is other-worldly. So pay attention to His advances. He rejoices when you glance His way.

THEY'RE PLAYING OUR SONG

I was riding on a chairlift at Keystone ski resort in Colorado. "Single," I had called out while standing in line—the proper etiquette for those skiing alone. No one took me up on the offer to share the chair...and I breathed a sigh of relief. I was alone. I was glad.

As the gears churned and the cables strained to pull my metal chair up the mountain, I sensed God's presence surrounding me. I wasn't alone after all. Wrapped in the down of His love and zipped up with the security of His grace, I settled in for the brisk morning ride. The great Rockies dressed in winter's garment of glistening snow stood tall all around me. Strong. Powerful. Majestic. Sure. The lapis vault of heaven canopied the earth with wisps of feathery brushstrokes. Delicate. Winsome. Graceful. Changing. It seemed as if the breath of God kissed my cheeks with the tingling crispness of that Colorado morning.

As the braids of metal drew me higher and higher, I heard a mother and her daughter in the chair behind me begin to sing. "Shout to the Lord, all the earth let us sing. Power and majesty praise to the king. Mountains bow down and the seas will roar at the sound of Your name."

Like an old couple that warms with remembrance when "their song" comes on the radio, I basked in knowing that God had specifically pushed G-5 on the jukebox just for me. For they were singing our song—God's and mine. It had been our song since I first heard the words in 1994. And it seemed God had just commissioned two of his children to serenade me. He was wooing me once again with music that wafted from behind and embraced my heart.

"He will take great delight in you, he will quiet you with his love, he will rejoice over you with singing" (Zephaniah 3:17). God sang His love song and I drank it in.

I closed my eyes, captivated by His evident love for me. A moment of sudden glory in the Rockies. I didn't want to get off the chairlift. I thought of Peter's words to Jesus after he had seen the transfiguration up on another high mountain two thousand years ago: "Lord, it is good for us to be here. If you wish, I will put up three shelters—one for you, one for Moses and one for Elijah" (Matthew 17:4). Like Peter, who had seen Jesus's sun-drenched face illuminate and His body clothed in light, I didn't want the moment to end. I wanted to pitch a tent and settle in. But just as Peter had to return to the valley below, I had to return to the flatlands.

Treks down the hill are always part of the mountain peak moments of sudden glory. That moment in the Rockies, when God wooed me with our love song through the timbre of two of his children, He was simply giving me another reminder of His love for me. *Remember,* He whispered.

"I have loved you with an everlasting love; I have drawn you with loving-kindness" (Jeremiah 31:3).

I slid off the chairlift and onto the snow-packed ramp. With a push of the poles and a dig of the skis, I headed back down the mountain once again. And our great love story continued from the peaks of the Rockies to the muddy, slushy slopes and masses of people below. God had pursued and romanced my heart once again.

God has pulled out all the stops in pursuit of your heart. But many, I dare say most, don't see it, don't hear it, and don't taste it. "Blessed are your eyes because they see," Jesus said, "and your ears because they hear" (Matthew 13:16).

We yearn to be cherished as a rare treasure. We dream of a love that is fresh every morning with anticipation of what the day may hold. We long for a love that will not wane with time or diminish with the doldrums of everyday life. And that is exactly what God wants to give you. I pray that you will hear God's love song and find His love notes lavishly tucked in the moments, that you will recognize the romance of God in the routine of your life. That is exactly what you can expect when *in Him we live and move and have our being* becomes a reality in your life. It is then that you experience a sacred union with God.

3

LIVING IN SACRED UNION

> He had prepared for you an abiding
> dwelling with Himself, where your whole
> life and every moment of it might be spent,
> where the world of your daily life might be
> done, and where all the while you might
> be enjoying unbroken communion with
> Himself.
>
> —ANDREW MURRAY, *Abide in Christ*

londin" was the stage name for Frenchman Jean-Francois
Gravelet. He was a fair-skinned, blue-eyed, blond-haired
young man who migrated to the United States with a troupe of
acrobats employed by Master Showman P. T. Barnum. In 1858, the
thirty-four-year-old Blondin visited Niagara Falls as a tourist and there
conceived the preposterous idea of walking across it. In his mind's
eye, he saw himself walking between the two countries—the United

States and Canada—over the great gorge on nothing more than a rope pathway taut between the two.

Harry Colcord became Blondin's agent and promoter, selling his product, "the Great Blondin!" And sell he did. On June 30, 1859, Blondin planned to make his first historic trek across the falls.

A 1,100-foot long, three-inch-diameter Manila rope stretched from one side of the gorge to the other. It sagged about twenty feet in the middle of the span and bounced about with the constant wind. This was not the usual tightrope act in a circus tent. The rope moved from side to side and up and down. There was no safety net.

Hundreds of men and women gathered to watch this incredible act of bravery—or madness; they didn't know which. With mingled emotions of fear and faith, the crowd watched as the acrobat stepped out in silk tights and a smile. A quarter of the way out over the great expanse, Blondin stopped, laid down on the rope, then appeared to take a quick nap. Ever the showman, he bounced up handlessly and proceeded to walk the rope. At one point, he even did a backflip and landed soundly on the rope to continue his jaunt. When he arrived triumphant on the Canadian side twenty minutes later, applause from both banks momentarily drowned out the roar of the falls.

Drenched in sweat, Blondin accepted a glass of champagne, did a little dance on the rope, and walked back across to the American side in a mere eight minutes. Those watching noted that Blondin appeared to be one with the rope. If the rope bounced, he bounced. If the rope swayed, he swayed.

As time passed, Blondin made many more crossings over Niagara Falls. Each crossing promised more aggressive and daring stunts: walking backward, walking on stilts, riding a bicycle, pushing a small stove in a wheelbarrow, and pausing to cook an omelet, and standing on his head in a chair. One day Blondin announced to his agent his intention to perform his most grand and daring stunt yet.

"Harry, here's a stunt that will complete our fortunes! I'll find a man and carry him over."

Colcord thought that was an ingenious idea and even offered a hefty sum to the man willing to be carried across the gorge. But after each man took one look at the treacherous churning water crashing on the rocks of the Falls, he quietly walked away.

But Blondin would not be undone. "Harry," he said, "You're a small man. I can carry you. Be a good fellow and come along."

Harry was speechless. Paying someone to be carried was one thing, but being carried himself was quite a different matter. In the end, Harry agreed. On August 17, 1859, the two men arrived on the Canadian side of Niagara Falls. Colcord, in a state of terror, hardly responded to Blondin as they approached the gorge, where the roiling water sped by at forty-two miles per hour. Blondin took Colcord by the hand and led him to the rope as one hundred thousand spectators looked on. Mechanically, Colcord mounted Blondin's back, wrapped his arms around his neck, and placed his feet into harnessed stirrups on either side of Blondin's hips. Colcord weighed 136 pounds, and the balancing pole weighed 40 pounds.

As Blondin stepped out onto the rope, Colcord grasped him so tightly he could barely breathe. Harry later recalled the moment:

Out over that horrible gulf I heard the roar of the water below and the hum which ran through the crowd. As we cleared the brink the hum ceased—the strain had spread to them.

Blondin walked on steadily, pausing for one brief moment at each point where the guy ropes joined the main cable. The line was a trifle steadier at these points.… Blondin halted at the last resting point before the middle span and yelled above the roar of water and wind, "Harry, you are no longer Colcord; you are Blondin. Until I clear this place be a part of me—mind, body, and soul. If I sway, sway with me. Do not attempt to do any balancing yourself. If you do we shall both go down to our death."[13]

From the ground, onlookers saw the pole tips, which usually moved slowly, were now whipping up and down "like the wings of a bird in rapid flight."

"Blondin was now running just as a boy runs in order to better keep his balance when walking on a railroad track," Colcord explained. "We were nearing the point where the joining place of the first guy-line from the opposite shore offered us a breathing space. Finally, Blondin's foot was planted on the knot that joined the lines. I was sucking in some air when suddenly the rope was jerked from beneath Blondin's feet."

Blondin maintained his balance and ran to the American soil. Cheers went up from both countries, and I imagine Colcord finally took that breath.

Isn't it interesting that every time Colcord tried to steady himself, he put the two of them in danger? Blondin knew the only way the pair would make it across the great chasm was if the two became one. Once Colcord quit struggling to maintain balance and the union was established, Blondin could carry him across safely. This, my friend, is a

picture of *in Him we live and move and have our being.* Colcord clinging to Blondin. Blondin wrapped in Colcord. Two becoming one...
union.

Why did I tell you this story? Because we are in a similar situation.
Just as Blondin carried Colcord, so Jesus carries us over the great gorge
we call life—from earth's soil to heaven's gate. When we try to balance on our own, we run the risk of tipping over into various Niagara
Falls of circumstances. We struggle and struggle, when the real work is
clinging to Jesus.

Jesus whispers, "Lean into me. Become one with me. Trust me to
get you there."

He is the showman. We are but the load.

"Jesus replied, This is the work (service) that God asks of you:
that you believe in the One Whom He has sent [that you cleave to,
trust, rely on, and have faith in His Messenger]" (John 6:29, AMP).
"This is the work," Jesus calls it. Our work is to believe, to trust. At
first glance that seems fairly easy. Like the backseat rider on a tandem
bicycle who rests her feet on the handlebars while the driver does all
the peddling. But I haven't met anyone yet who relinquishes control
and completely trusts with ease. Trusting, resting, giving up control goes
against our natural bent. But isn't our natural bent what Jesus came to
save us from?

Paul wrote: "But the person who is joined to the Lord is one spirit
with him" (1 Corinthians 6:17, NLT). Jesus doesn't want us simply to
follow after Him. He wants us to be in union with Him. I believe there
is a big difference. *In* Him we live and move and have our being, not
behind Him.

FROM FOLLOWING TO ABIDING

"Follow me," Jesus called as He walked along the path of life and invited holy hitchhikers to join Him in the greatest adventure of all time. "Come, follow me," He called to the sons of Zebedee, James and John (Matthew 4:21). "Follow me," He called out to Matthew and Philip (Matthew 9:9; John 1:43). "Follow me," He invited the rich young ruler (Matthew 19:21). Some accepted the invitation, others did not.

But in Jesus's final words to his eleven best friends, I see a different sort of invitation: "Remain in me, and I will remain in you," He urged (John 15:4). Another translation says it this way: "Dwell in Me and I will dwell in you. [Live in Me, and I will live in you]" (AMP). And still another says: "Abide in Me, and I in you" (NASB). Jesus invited the disciples to *follow after Him* while here on earth. The night before He faced the cross, He invited them to *abide in Him* after he was gone. That is quite a difference. No longer is one person following behind another, but the two become one and move as one. I in Him and He in me; that is the beauty of the sacred union.

When I was a child, I remember hearing that we could have Jesus in our hearts. However, for every one time the Bible talks about having Jesus in you, there are ten times that say you are in Jesus. When I think of Jesus in me, the idea seems quite small. He goes where I go. However, when I think of me in Jesus, that is a much bigger picture. I go where He goes!

I am in Jesus and He is in me. We've moved from following behind to abiding in. Maybe I'm splitting hairs, but in my mind's eye, this seems to be very different. When I think of "following," I don't have a picture of union. When I think of "abiding," I picture two moving as one.

I think the concept of abiding is a difficult one. We understand "follow me" much easier than "abide in me." Following provides a physical picture that is easy to grasp. Abiding is a spiritual concept that requires a spiritual acuity.

Dwelling in Christ does not mean coming into His presence for times of Bible study and prayer and then walking out of His presence in order to attend to the mundane duties of life that take up the greater part of your day. Your relationship with Jesus is not meant to be experienced in little puffs that refresh for a moment but in the continual breathing in and out of His presence. Abiding. Union. Moving as one.

Consider these words Jesus spoke to His disciples as He explained what would happen after his death and resurrection: "On that day you will realize that I am in my Father, and you are in me, and I am in you" (John 14:20). Is that difficult to visualize? Try this: Write Jesus's name on a little card and place that card in an envelope. Write your name on that envelope. There you have Jesus in you.

Now take that envelope and put it into a larger envelope. Write Jesus's name on the larger envelope. Now you have Jesus in you, and you in Jesus.

Finally, place all of that in an even larger envelope and write "God" on the outside. Now you have Jesus in you, you in Jesus, and all that in God. "On that day you will realize that I am in my Father, and you are in me, and I am in you"...union. "In Christ" is your new address—it is where you live, and it is how you live.

SEPARATING WHAT WE FEEL FROM WHAT WE KNOW

You are a triune being with a body, soul, and spirit. Within your soul you have a mind, will, and emotions. You have feelings, and most likely you long to feel close to God. And if you are like most people, sometimes you feel closer to God than other times.

Sometimes I feel closer to my husband than other times. But that doesn't mean I'm any less married at some times than others. I usually feel closer to him after we've enjoyed a fun time together, been especially intimate, or gone through a struggle where we've locked arms and walked through it together.

It's not that much different in my relationship with God. I might *feel* closer to Him when we've had a good time together (as in worship service), been especially intimate spiritually (as in a morning quiet time), or gone through a struggle where we've locked arms and walked through the difficulty together (as in mourning the death of a loved one).

But just because I *feel* closer to God in a particular moment doesn't mean that I am. It is just a feeling. We know that we cannot have that giddy feeling about our spouse all the time. Then why do we think we have to have that with God?

Paul prayed for the Ephesians that the God of our Lord Jesus Christ would give them the Spirit of wisdom and revelation so that they could *know* him better…that they might *know* the hope to which he had called them (see Ephesians 1:17–19). He prayed for the Colossians that they would "*know* the mystery of God, namely, Christ, in whom are hidden all the treasures of wisdom and knowledge" (Colossians

2:2–3). He did not pray that they would *feel* like they were close to God or *feel* the love of God. He prayed that they would *know* it.

Specifically, Paul prayed:

> I pray that out of his glorious riches he may strengthen you
> with power through his Spirit in your inner being, so that
> Christ may dwell in your hearts through faith. [How? Through
> faith. In your "knower."] And I pray that you, being rooted and
> established in love, may have power, together with all the saints,
> to grasp how wide and long and high and deep is the love of
> Christ, and to *know* this love that surpasses knowledge—that
> you may be filled to the measure of all the fullness of God.
> (Ephesians 3:16–19)

Why do we experience times when we feel far from God? How can we feel far from God if His Holy Spirit lives in us? If you are in Christ and He is in you, why don't you feel Him at all times? Can you feel distant from your liver, from your kidney, or from your pancreas? Being near to God, or rather *feeling* near to God, is not a matter of proximity, as if one of us moved closer or farther away. It is not a matter of a physical position, but it is a matter of our relational acuity. It is a spiritual receptivity, a spiritual awareness, and a spiritual acknowledgment of His presence.

Charles Spurgeon once said: "It may be that there are saints who are always at their best, and are happy enough never to lose the light of their Father's countenance. I am not sure that there are such persons.... I have not traversed that happy land. Every year of my life has had a winter as well as a summer, and every single day has its night.... I confess that though the substance be in us, as in the teil-tree and the oak, yet we do lose our leaves, and the sap within us does not flow with equal vigor at all seasons."[14]

God has promised He will never leave us, but we can feel far from Him when we ignore Him, live independently from Him, or rush about expecting Him to tag along rather than move in union with Him where He leads.

And while your humanness falters between spiritual times of plenty and times of want, communion with God is always just a whisper away as you acknowledge His presence with you and in you.

A MOMENT-BY-MOMENT DECISION

Abiding in, dwelling in, remaining in Christ all sound like wonderful ideas. I'm sure you'd agree there is no place we'd rather be. But what does that look like...really...practically? Busy: now we know what that looks like. We complain about being *too* busy, but I think we actually revel in it. We like being busy for God because, if we're honest, it makes us feel like we matter. After all, where would God be without our help? Where would He be without us? Right? (Of course, I'm jesting here.)

We work and we work and we work. Striving for what we already have. However, a filled calendar does not reflect a fulfilled life. Have you ever walked into a nursery full of toddlers? They are definitely busy, but to what end? They aren't being very productive but making a big mess instead. I fear many of us are like those toddlers moving from one toy to the next, one activity to the next, one distraction to the next...but we're not accomplishing much that matters in the process.

Jesus began his lesson in John 15 by comparing our lives to that of a branch attached to or "abiding" on a vine.

> "I am the true vine, and my Father is the gardener.... Remain in me, and I will remain in you. No branch can bear fruit by itself; it must remain in the vine. Neither can you bear fruit unless you remain in me. I am the vine; you are the branches. If a man remains in me and I in him, he will bear much fruit; apart from me you can do nothing" (verses 1, 4–5).

You can be busy in work of your own making apart from God's desire for you, but that busyness won't amount to much of eternal value. Work that does not flow out of worship remains just that: work. If our serving does not come from the overflow of our abiding in Christ, we will feel drained quickly. But when our activity flows out of a full heart that results from our sacred union, we may be tired, but not depleted. And we will bear much fruit in the process.

When a branch is grafted onto a vine, both must be injured. The vine is wounded or cut open to receive the branch. The branch is wounded or cut off from its original life source. And then the two are joined at the raw openings. Oh, do you see it? Jesus was wounded, cut open, laid bare. Then we are cut off from our old life of sin and grafted onto Him. Wound to wound. Death to life. This union was costly, and I am again amazed at the price Jesus paid for me.

In John 15, Jesus told the disciples to *abide* or *remain* in Him about ten times (depending on which translation you read). Why did He repeat that ten times in ten sentences? Because He knew abiding or union would not come naturally.

When Jesus tells us to "abide," He is speaking to our mind, will, and emotions. Abiding is a moment-by-moment decision. So how can you "abide in Christ" and attend to life at the same time? There's only one way: by erasing the lines between the secular and the sacred. When you *live and move and have your being* in Jesus, every aspect of your life, even the places of your mundane activities, will be transformed into holy ground, filled with moments of sudden glory. Union. It's the only way.

Monasteries were begun by men who wanted to focus all their attention on union with Christ. But even monks have to grow food, pay bills, and peel potatoes. Jesus tells us to be in the world but not of the world. Abiding doesn't mean we separate ourselves out of the world to live a life of solitary meditation and contemplation. Where is the fruit in that? Even Jesus moved among the multitudes. He still does. He does it through men and women who understand what it means *to live and move and have their being in Him.*

Andrew Murray wrote the following about abiding in Christ:

It was not to refresh you for a few short hours after your conversion with the joy of His love and deliverance, and then to send you forth to wander in sadness and sin. He has destined you to something better than a short-lived blessedness, to be enjoyed only in times of special earnestness and prayer, and then to pass away, as you had to return to those duties in which far the greater part of life has to be spent.

No indeed; He had prepared for you an abiding dwelling with Himself, where your whole life and every moment of it might be spent, where the work of your daily life might be done, and where all the while you might be enjoying unbroken communion with Himself.[15]

ERASING THE LINES
BETWEEN THE SACRED AND THE SECULAR

"I just never have enough time to spend with the Lord," Amanda cries. "I work forty-plus hours a week, commute ninety minutes both ways, oversee elderly parents' affairs, and take care of my five-year-old son. I'm either on the road, at my desk, or taking care of someone else's needs. And on top of that, I never feel like I'm doing any of it well. What does God want from me in the middle of all this madness? How can I carve out time for Him? I feel like I'm constantly failing Him!"

Amanda is not alone. I've been right there with her. Haven't you?

We live in a physical realm, and our new, born-again spirits will never be completely satisfied here on earth. There will always be tension between the two. Living in union with the Spirit of God is counterintuitive to the ways of this world. What causes that tension and prevents us from experiencing unbroken union with Christ? I believe it is the tendency to compartmentalize life into two hemispheres: the secular and the sacred.

Everyday secular activities vie for our attention, while our times of worship and communion are relegated to Sunday morning worship, early morning quiet times, and midweek Bible studies (if we can fit them in). We spend the majority of our days operating in secular, day-to-day activities and feeling guilty for the lack of time spent in sacred communion with God. And for most of us, a struggle to find the balance between the secular and the sacred wages war in our hearts. We live in the secular and yet long to be in the sacred. The constant flip-flopping between the two is exhausting, and inevitably we see one as the winner and one as the loser. We see ourselves as failures struggling to get out of Romans 7 and longing to live in Romans 8. We wobble on a spiritual tightrope, fearing the slightest misstep will toss us into the canyon of God's disapproval.

Thankfully, there is a way to wave the white flag of surrender and end the battle's constant conflict. We can experience true union with Christ when we erase the dividing line and meld the two.

What would that look like? Let's go back to Amanda.

What if Amanda communed with God *while* she commuted to work? *While* she worked at her job? *While* she took care of her family? Do you see how that would help alleviate the false guilt that adds to her feelings of insufficiency?

The physical or secular realm involves cooking, cleaning, ironing, shopping, vacuuming, laundering smelly clothes, washing dirty faces, and wiping messy bottoms. It involves being a wife, a mother, an employee, an employer, a friend, a student, and a host of other roles and responsibilities that merge on any given day. What could be sacred about all that? Everything. But we'll get to that in a minute.

The spiritual or sacred realm includes praying, reading the Bible, going to church, memorizing scripture, serving the poor, and meditating on meaningful messages. The spiritual aspects of our lives include worship and practicing spiritual disciplines.

I want to suggest that God never intended for the lines separating the secular and the sacred to exist in the first place. If *in Him we live and move and have our being* is true in your life, then the sacred also includes cooking, cleaning, ironing, shopping, vacuuming, laundering smelly clothes, washing dirty faces, and wiping messy bottoms. When you erase the lines between the secular and the sacred, your entire life can become an act of worship.

How do you put this into practice? By merging the two worlds.

Suppose you merge the secular and the sacred into one God-glorifying life. Suppose you acknowledge God's presence as you walk down the grocery store aisle, drive through the carpool line, sit in the hair stylist's chair, stir the spaghetti sauce, shampoo your hair, love your husband, or rake leaves in the yard. Isn't that what *in Him we live and move and have our being* really looks like? Praying with your eyes wide open at times is the only way to practice prayer without ceasing.

Monday always follows Sunday, but when you erase the lines that separate the secular and the sacred, the world becomes your sanctuary. God's presence becomes one steady stream.

This was true for Jesus. He never hurried. He never panicked. He was never driven by the tyranny of the urgent. If I were in His sandals, I probably would have been wringing my hands with all I had to accomplish in three-and-a-half years. I can hear myself now: "I've got three-and-a-half years to make a difference. How can I cram all the miracles and teaching into this short amount of time?"

Three-and-a-half years translates into 1,278 days. If you go back and count the days recorded in the four gospels, you'd come up considerably short. So what was Jesus doing on the days that were not mentioned by Matthew, Mark, Luke, and John? He lived His life. He worked. He ate. He washed. He partied. He prayed. He studied. He meditated. He listened. The Sacred lived in the midst of the secular.

When we see our work as something we do solely for others, we tend to expect appreciation or wait for applause...and we can become *we wait for appreciation from others*

bitter when neither come. "Her children rise up and bless her." But sometimes they don't. "Her husband also, and he praises her" (Proverbs 31:28, NASB). But more often than not he doesn't. *Humph,* we huff as we stew in our own joyless juices of duty. But if we see our work as unto the Lord—as sacred—then "Well done, good and faithful servant!" (Matthew 25:21) becomes our greatest joy.

Paul wrote: "Whether, then, you eat or drink or whatever you do, do all to the glory of God" (1 Corinthians 10:31, NASB). *Whatever you do…*

Cleaning bathrooms to the glory of God.

Vacuuming the floor to the glory of God.

Reading my Bible to the glory of God.

Singing praises to the glory of God.

Being intimate with my husband to the glory of God.

Cooking dinner to the glory of God.

Helping in the soup kitchen to the glory of God.

Shopping for groceries to the glory of God.

Mailing packages to the glory of God.

Filing my taxes to the glory of God.

All things…to the glory of God.

Writing a book to the Glory of God

What does "to the glory of God" mean? As mentioned in chapter 1, the Greek word for "glory" is *doxa* and denotes honor or splendor, a reflection of God's character. We are to reflect God's character, His ways, and His splendor in *everything* we do. Discounting sinful behavior, such as sexual perversions, gossip, drug and alcohol abuse, or any number of immoral acts that contradict the life of a Christian, our entire existence both in the secular and the sacred realm could and should be an act of worship. When that happens, goals such as "do everything as unto the Lord" and "pray without ceasing" become clearer and more within our grasp.

Yes, we do need times alone with God. Jesus pulled away to be with the Father often. "Very early in the morning, while it was still dark, Jesus got up, left the house and went off to a solitary place, where he prayed" (Mark 1:35). If Jesus, the Son of God, needed to spend extended time alone with his Father, then we certainly do too. However, by acknowledging God's presence in every aspect of our lives, we will experience the blessed union in all things. Moments of sudden glory will appear as manna from God.

God longs for you to experience His presence in the spin of the laundry, the sizzle of the cooking, the buzz of children's chatter, and in the quiet of solitude. From the time God rent the curtain in the holy of holies when Jesus took His last breath on the cross, God welcomed you into His presence…not just on so-called holy days, but everyday days.

PEELING POTATOES FOR THE GLORY OF GOD

Brother Lawrence was a man who intentionally erased the dividing lines of secular and sacred. Lawrence loved God and wanted to dedicate his entire life to study and worship. He joined a monastery, where he was expected to spend three hours a day in prayer. However, he often spent his entire prayer time trying to stay focused, "rejecting stray thoughts and falling back into them again."[16] He felt his mind was tossed like a vessel in the storm abandoned by its pilot. I've been on that ship. Haven't you?

Lawrence's solution to the inner turmoil was to drop anchor on a habit of continual conversation with God. Whether he was at work or in prayer, he determined to focus his heart and mind on God—thanking Him, praising Him, and asking for grace to do whatever had to be done. And if his mind veered off course and forgot God for even a moment, he confessed and drew his thoughts back to God like a prodigal returning home.

I admire Brother Lawrence for his honesty in admitting his difficulty in staying focused during extended times of prayer. It is refreshing… freeing, really. And here I thought I was the only one. Not really. I know many people share the same struggle.

I imagine Brother Lawrence had great expectations when he joined the monastery. A life devoted to focusing on God! Escaping the outside world and living among other like-minded saints who were totally devoted to God. It sounds like a dream come true!

And where did his superiors place this holy man? What was his lot in this new life of worship? In the kitchen. Oh, I feel his frustration!

So off Brother Lawrence went to the kitchen to become the chief cook and bottle washer for his band of brothers. His duties also included shopping and negotiating for the monastery's various enterprises, such as winery sales. His tasks seemed neither holy nor heavenly.

But one day he decided he was going to put on a new set of lenses from which to view his tasks. Rather than complain about his lot in this life, he was going to merge the secular and the sacred. He made a choice to do "all to the glory of God," and before he knew it, the mundane chores became acts of worship. And that made all the difference. He spent the last forty years of his life in a moment-by-moment adventure of practicing the presence of God by merging the secular and the sacred into one. He admitted that he never looked forward to the imposed prayer retreats because they did not focus him more on God than doing his busiest work.

Brother Lawrence practiced journaling before *journaling* was even a word. I would love to see his writings, but most of them he tore up and threw away because he felt his writings were so inferior to what he was experiencing inwardly with God. His journaling was merely an outlet to relieve the fullness of his heart, to pour out what God had put in, in order to receive yet again. I suspect he was no stranger to "sudden glory" moments.

Brother Lawrence worshiped God while peeling potatoes, tending the vineyard, and kneeling on the bench in prayer. There was no distinction and no more importance placed on one than the other. He *lived and moved and had his being* in God. Prayer without ceasing. Glorifying God in all things. A genuine inloveness. Sacred union.

TWO BECOMING ONE

Marriage has been called the human echo of Christ and the Church. It is an earthly picture of the union we experience as we *live and move and have our being* in Jesus—the truest of holy matrimony and sacred wedlock. This union does not negate who you are but actually makes you more fully who you were created to be as you reflect God's glory.

Let's take one more peek into Sheldon Vanauken's relationship with his wife, Davy, as he paints a beautiful picture of the union they shared.

If one of us likes *anything,* there must be something to like in it—and the other one must find it. Every single thing that either of us likes. That way we shall create a thousand strands, great and small, that will link us together. Then we shall be so close that it would be impossible—unthinkable—for either of us to suppose that we could ever recreate such closeness with anyone else. And our trust in each other will not only be based on love and loyalty but on *the fact* of a thousand sharings—a thousand strands twisted into something unbreakable.[17]

Can you see it? What a beautiful description of our union that takes place—or could take place—with Jesus. When you erase the lines between the secular and the sacred, every experience is a shared experience. Every moment holds within it the possibility of a sudden glory. "And our trust in each other will not only be based on love and loyalty but on *the fact* of a thousand sharings—a thousand strands twisted into something unbreakable."

Over the past fifty years or so, I've noticed a trend among married women. Rather than taking their husband's last name, some simply add their husband's name to their own, adjoining the two with a hyphen and keeping theirs intact. Mary Smith becomes Mary Smith-Jones. Betty James becomes Betty James-Riley.

Now I know there are a plethora of reasons for having a hyphenated last name. And I know there may be a multitude of opinions on the subject. I'm not here to voice an opinion about the trend itself, but I do have an opinion about how it mirrors the way many folks view their relationship with Jesus. Hyphenated Christians abound.

I have to ask myself, am I a hyphenated Christian? Have I simply tacked Jesus onto my already busy life? Have I tacked the title "Christian" onto the long list of words that describe who I am and what I believe? Is Jesus just another add-on? Is He an app I've down-loaded for easy access? Have I taken on Jesus's name to some extent but kept my own identity unchanged? Jesus would have thought that preposterous. He said, "I am in my Father, and you are in me, and I am in you" (John 14:20).

Becoming a Christian is serious business. It is an all-or-nothing proposition, and I fear we have watered it down to simply something we add on to our already busy lives. Jesus is not someone you add to your life. When you come to Him, He becomes your life.

C. S. Lewis notes the following about the Christian life:

> Christ says, "Give me All. I don't want so much of your time and so much of your money and so much of your work: I want *you.* I have not come to torment your natural self, but to kill it. No half-measures are any good. I don't want to cut off a branch here and a branch there; I want to have the whole tree down.... Hand over the whole natural self, all the desires which you think innocent as well as the ones you think wicked—the whole outfit. I will give you a new self instead. In fact, I will give you Myself: my own will shall become yours."[18]

Jesus warned those who were considering becoming one of His disciples. "If anyone would come after me, he must deny himself and take up his cross and follow me. For whoever wants to save his life will lose it, but whoever loses his life for me will find it" (Matthew 16:24–25).

Eugene Peterson paraphrases Jesus's words in Matthew 7:13–14 this way:

Don't look for shortcuts to God. The market is flooded with surefire, easygoing formulas for a successful life that can be practiced in your spare time. Don't fall for that stuff, even though crowds of people do. The way to life—to God!—is vigorous and requires total attention" (MSG).

A little bit of sugar might make the medicine go down, but a little bit of Jesus will not satisfy the glory ache in us. True union with Jesus is an all-exclusive relationship.

Imagine if your husband had proposed marriage to you with the following caveat: "Dear one, I love you and adore you. I want to spend the rest of my life with you. I promise to be faithful to you 360 days a year. But I do have this thing for blondes, and well, you are a brunette. So five days of the year, I'll keep to myself. But the other 360 days, I'm all yours!"

I don't know which cheek I'd slap first, the right or the left. But I do know that man's ring would not go on my finger.

Making Jesus not only Savior but also Lord of your life involves a certain exclusivity that is somewhat similar to marriage but unmistakably unique to any human relationship. The union involves our entire being, and not one molecule goes unaffected. This relationship is all-exclusive, meaning that it excludes every other possible "god" that you could place upon the throne of your life, and it is all-inclusive, meaning there is no part of your life in which Jesus does not rule. When true union takes place, a certain sweetness flavors all of life.

Jesus said, "Make your home in me just as I do in you" (John 15:4, MSG). "These words I speak to you are not incidental additions to your life, homeowner improvements to your standard of living.

They are foundational words, words to build a life on" (Matthew 7:24, MSG).

Our sinful nature clings to individuality and fights against union. *Me, my,* and *mine* are the mantra of the flesh. In the Bible, Jesus said this of marriage: "The two will become one" (Matthew 19:5), but I imagine many stand at the altar and wonder, "Yeah, but which one?"

Listen to the words Jesus prayed for you and for me:

> Holy Father, protect them [the disciples] by the power of your name—the name you gave me—so that they may be *one* as we are *one.*... My prayer is not for them alone. I pray also for those who will believe in me through their message [me and you], that all of them may be *one,* Father, just as you are in me and I am in you. May they also be in us so that the world may believe that you have sent me. I have given them the glory that you gave me, that they may be *one* as we are *one:* I in them and you in me. May they be brought to complete unity to let the world know that you sent me and have loved them even as you have loved me" (John 17:11, 20–23).

If you really want to experience true union with Jesus, you must drop the hyphen. He's not an add-on to your life. He *is* your life.

Hanging On for Dear Life

Steven was just a preschooler when I first taught him to snow ski. The very first day was arduous—for me. I felt like a down-covered workhorse as I lugged two sets of skis in one arm while dragging

Steven along with the other. Clunky ski boots, overstuffed mittens, and a hooded snowsuit made it difficult for Steven to maneuver. Add all that to the slippery snow, long lift lines, and a resistant four-year-old, and you have the makings for a windfall of whining in a winter wonderland.

After several failed attempts to teach Steven how to snowplow down the bunny slope with the ski tips pointed inward, I came up with another idea. I made an A-frame tent with my legs. Then Steven stood in front and between them. He wrapped his arms around my thighs, and off we went! He went where I went. If I moved right, he moved right. If I moved left, he moved left. His only responsibility was to hang on and relinquish control. And even though he thought he was skiing, in reality he was simply along for the ride.

What a picture of how I want my journey with God to be. I cling to Him, wrap my arms around Him, and move where He moves. If He goes left, I go left. If He goes right, I go right. "But the person who is joined to the Lord is one spirit with him" (1 Corinthians 6:17, NLT).

King David wrote, "I cling to you; your strong right hand holds me securely" (Psalm 63:8, NLT). Peterson's paraphrase says it this way: "I hold on to you for dear life" (MSG). I see Blondin and Colcord. I see Jesus and me. Union. A sudden glory.

JOINING GOD
IN CONTINUAL CONVERSATION

> The weight of God's glory…daily and
> everywhere, punctures earth's lid and
> heaven falls through the holes.
> —ANN VOSKAMP, *One Thousand Gifts*

*T*he sun had not pried open the day quite yet. We had been traveling for several days, going from one Pacific island to another, and I had not been able to sleep the night before. While I had enjoyed seeing God's creation, I had missed our times alone—just the two of us.

Wrapped in a blanket with a hot cup of coffee, I snuck away with my Beloved for a quiet rendezvous before others in the house stirred. As I gazed out through sliding glass doors, I drank in the view of the stilled Pacific Ocean spread before me. All seemed gray in this predawn expanse of sky and sea.

I grabbed my Bible, and it fell open to the middle. I didn't bother to turn the pages. I looked down and read familiar words from the well-worn love letter: "May God be gracious to us and bless us and make his face shine upon us" (Psalm 67:1). When I looked up, I noticed the sun struggling to send its rays through two small openings in the early morning clouds...two holes side by side, like headlights on high beam. As I continued watching the morning sun stretch its arms of light, another break in the clouds provided a slit for the rays to escape. An upturned crescent emerged directly under the two circular beams above. And then I saw it—a celestial smiley face beaming through the clouds...divine delight...a holy grin! God's radiant smile welcomed me to another day.

I had a front row seat in God's theater as His glory pierced the darkness and spilled forth grace that filled my heart. Once again, while I rose to pursue Him, He beat me to the punch and reminded me that He was the one pursuing me. I simply showed up. Ah, sometimes we simply need to show up.

God had made His "face shine upon me," and my smile, be it ever so small and unassuming, mirrored His gift to me. As if the words in His love letter weren't enough, He wrote them in the sky like a love-struck beau. His passionate pursuit amazed me once again, and I was drawn like a moth to the flame of His love. Me—the bride pursued.

Months later, I told a friend about that precious moment God and I shared on that small Pacific Island so far away from home.

"Things like that never happen to me," she sighed.

"Oh, yes they do," I corrected. "You just need to learn how to recognize them."

And I believe that with all my heart. This is worth saying again: God has pulled out all the stops to reveal glimpses of His glory. But many, I dare say most, don't see it, don't hear it, and don't taste it. "Blessed are your eyes because they see," Jesus said, "and your ears because they hear" (Matthew 13:16).

How God Reveals Glimpses of Glory

All day long God speaks to us, but it is up to us to listen. He speaks through His Word, the Holy Spirit, prayer, other people, nature, and circumstances. I revel in those words in Genesis that tell of God walking with Adam and Eve in the cool of the day. Haven't you longed to take such a walk with God? to hear His voice? to see His footprints alongside your path?

As I turn the pages of my Bible, I see God speaking audibly to Noah, telling him to build an ark; to Rebekah, foretelling the future of her twin boys; to Moses, calling him to lead the enslaved Israelites out of Egypt; to the prophet Samuel, leading him to anoint a mere shepherd boy the next king of Israel; to Hagar, as she ran away from her difficult mistress. Haven't you longed for God to speak to you in the same way?

And yet, He does speak to you and me. He may not speak audibly to us, but He does speak. Sometimes we simply don't know how to detect that still small voice that gives us constant reminders of His presence and involvement in our lives. But when we understand *in Him we live and move and have our being*, when we understand the uniqueness of living in sacred union, continual conversation moves back and forth in a steady ebb and flow. We talk to God. God talks to us. We listen to God. God listens to us. Glory moments abound. "Over here!" He calls. "Take a look at this! I've planned this display of My glory just for you!"

Perhaps you've thought, *If I could just get away from the hustle and bustle of everyday life, then maybe I could hear from God.* But as I've studied Scripture, I've noticed some of God's most memorable conversations were conducted while men and women were not on a spiritual retreat but right smack-dab in the middle of their busy lives. He spoke to Moses while he was tending sheep, to Gideon while he was threshing wheat, to the Samaritan woman while she was drawing water for her daily chores, to John while he was fishing, to Peter while he was napping (well, maybe not so busy), and to Martha while she was baking in the kitchen.

There are some who say that God does not speak today. They argue that the Bible is God's complete revelation to believers. But it was Jesus who said, "I am the good shepherd.... My sheep listen to my voice; I know them, and they follow me" (John 10:14, 27). Again, it is not a matter of whether or not God speaks today; it is a matter of whether we will listen to the Shepherd calling our names.

The cacophony in our cluttered world makes it difficult to detect His still small voice. The din is compounded by the constant e-mails, texts, instant messaging, tweets, and cell phones that vie for our attention. Did I mention constant? I got tickled when I read A. W. Tozer's commentary on the devices that competed with God's voice in his day, 1955:

Modern civilization is so complex as to make the devotional life all but impossible. It wears us out by multiplying distractions and beats us down by destroying our solitude, where otherwise we might drink and renew our strength before going out to face the world again.... 'Commune with your own heart upon your bed and be still' is a wise and healing counsel, but how can it be followed in this day of the newspaper, the telephone, the radio and the television? These modern playthings, like pet tiger cubs, have grown so large and dangerous that they threaten to devour us all.... No spot is now safe from the world's intrusion.[19]

Oh, Mr. Tozer, if you could see us now. Tiger cubs have grown into ravenous beasts that run wild and thrive on a steady diet of silence and solitude, which they gobble up and devour at will. But despite the tiger cubs of our day, moments of sudden glory to soothe the ache are still possible, if we will but turn aside and pay attention.

Moses was taking care of sheep when he noticed a burning bush that was not being consumed. He stopped what he was doing and walked over to investigate. "When the LORD saw that he turned aside to look, God called to him from the midst of the bush and said, 'Moses, Moses!' And he said, 'Here I am'" (Exodus 3:4, NASB).

Ah, *when he turned aside.* Could it be that we are so busy bustling about that we don't turn aside to listen? to notice? Could it be that we don't slow down enough to investigate as a sleuthing child expecting Him to speak? Could it be that we have so compartmentalized our lives into the secular and the sacred that we falsely think that God would only speak during times of quiet solitude or through the words of a pastor or teacher? Glory moments abound when we tune into God's frequency and listen for the timbre of His voice. As Elizabeth Barrett Browning said: "Earth is crammed with heaven and every common bush afire with God. But only he who sees, takes off his shoes."[20]

The gift of sudden-glory moments becomes secondary as the realization of who sends them becomes primary. "I AM WHO I AM" (Exodus 3:14). Ah, the glory Sender has a name. He wants to speak to you in intimate relationship.

Once God spoke to Moses, it only salted his thirst to know Him more. He wasn't satisfied with this one-time encounter at the burning bush. He prayed, "If you are pleased with me, teach me your ways so I may know you and continue to find favor with you" (Exodus 33:13). I wonder, if God had spoken to me from a burning bush, if I would have been satisfied with that one incident, or would it have sparked a desire to know Him more? Sometimes I fear we stop too soon; we are satisfied with the prologue when multiple chapters are yet to be recorded on our hearts.

When your union with God is restored through your relationship with Jesus, when *in Him we live and move and have our being* becomes a reality in your life, your ears will hear, your eyes will see, and your senses will detect the glory of the Lord turning ordinary days into extraordinary treasures. The Holy Spirit takes up residence (1 Corinthians 3:16) and tunes our senses to experience moments of sudden glory through the Bible, through prayer, through circumstances, and through other people. However, each time we ignore or resist the Spirit (Acts 7:51), grieve the Spirit (Ephesians 4:30), or quench the Spirit (1 Thessalonians 5:19, NASB), we decrease our spiritual acuity to hear from Him. Each time we resist Him, it is as if we've turned down the volume of His voice. The Holy Spirit will not leave us, but if we neglect Him or refuse to listen, His voice can grow dim. Yes, God speaks in various ways, but the Holy Spirit is the conduit through which those glory moments flow.

All day long God lavishes you with ceaseless caresses, recurring reminders, and simple surprises, if you will but turn aside to see. A good day becomes not one in which the to-do list is sufficiently checked but one in which you've stayed in touch with Him and gathered the bouquet of glory moments waiting to be picked.

Our faithful God has not changed. He still speaks to us. We should never try to determine exactly *how* He will speak, just *that* He will speak. Exactly how and when He makes Himself known will be as creative as He is—infinitely so. But be assured of this: He is continuously speaking and uniquely articulate.

SUDDEN GLORY MOMENTS THROUGH THE BIBLE

While God speaks and reveals His glory in a variety of ways through a variety of means, He will never tell us anything that contradicts His Word—the Bible.

Timothy wrote, "All Scripture is God-breathed" (2 Timothy 3:16). Some translations use the word *inspired.* The Greek word for "God-breathed" is *theopneustos* and implies much more than being merely inspired. It is God's very words breathed into men's hearts and transcribed by men's fingers. God spoke the words; men simply wrote them down. As I mentioned in chapter 1, the Hebrew word for "Scripture" is *mikra,* and means "the calling out of God." He calls out to us from the pages and speaks to us though the words.

One day I was reading John chapter 20. I imagined myself standing with Mary Magdalene before the empty tomb, then running back with her to tell the disciples of her astounding discovery. I envisioned myself kneeling beside her weeping form as Jesus called out her name. "Mary." These were words I had read before, but God had a surprise for me just around the corner. As I continued reading about Jesus's resurrection, I pictured myself pulling up a chair with the disciples as Jesus suddenly appeared in their secret hideaway.

> On the evening of that first day of the week, when the disciples were together, with the doors locked for fear of the Jews, Jesus came and stood among them and said, "Peace be with you!" After he said this, he showed them his hands and side. The disciples were overjoyed when they saw the Lord. (verses 19–20)

I sensed God telling me to pay attention. To stop and picture the scene, not just read it. And as I peered into the room with my spiritual eyes, I saw something that I had never seen before. The disciples did not recognize Jesus. They didn't know who He was… until they saw His scars. Once they saw His hands and side, they knew it was Him.

Then God began to speak to me through this story. *Sharon, you've seen it. The disciples did not recognize Jesus until they saw His scars, and that is still how the world recognizes Jesus today…when My people are not ashamed to show their scars.*

This was a moment of sudden glory that changed my life and my ministry forever. He showed me the power and purpose behind the scars in my own life: to help others recognize Jesus. The scars of my past (and your past) are not something to be ashamed of. They tell a story. A story of wounds healed by the Healer. They tell of Jesus's power at work in our lives.

Like perusing an art museum filled with masterpieces, I had stopped to ponder one particular painting, and a story began to unfold with colors and hues I had never noticed before. It was a sudden glory that took my breath away.

If you've never experienced God speaking to you through the pages of the Bible, I encourage you to ask Him to take you into the story and make it come alive for you. This is the only book you will ever read where the author is always present. He is right there with you and would love to speak to you personally and open your eyes to new truths you've never seen before. He longs to give you moments of sudden glory as He makes His presence known through the Scriptures.

While God speaks to you through the Bible, it is the Holy Spirit who opens your eyes to see and your ears to hear. Without the work of the Holy Spirit, the words on the pages of Scripture will remain simply words. Just as a seed cannot germinate and grow in the earth without water, the seeds of Scripture cannot germinate and grow in your heart without the Spirit. It is the Holy Spirit who awakens your spirit to sense God's presence and detect that still small voice (see 1 Corinthians 3:16).

SUDDEN GLORY MOMENTS THROUGH PRAYER

We saw in chapter 3 how Brother Lawrence erased the lines between the secular and the sacred to practice continual conversation with God and prayer without ceasing. But God also speaks to us in specific times of extended prayer. Jesus said, "But when you pray, go into your room, close the door and pray to your Father, who is unseen" (Matthew 6:6).

Prayer is communion and communication with God. For us, as God's children, prayer includes praising God for who He is, thanking Him for what He does, confessing our sin, asking for forgiveness, petitioning God for our requests, and interceding for others. It is also listening for God's response.

Prayer is not a wish list for a celestial Santa Claus. It is not our to-do list for God. I sometimes cringe at the self-centered and self-focused way we tend to approach the God of all creation. Extended times of prayer are not meant to change God's mind but to align our thinking with His. Jesus never set His agenda and then asked God to bless it. He only did what the Father told Him to do (John 5:19). The Father told Jesus to go to Samaria, to the next town, and to Zacchaeus's home for dinner. He also directed Jesus to delay His journey to see His ailing friend, Lazarus, delay His appearance at the festival, and shake the dust off His feet as He left His unbelieving hometown. Jesus spent extended time in prayer before He chose His disciples, before He made travel plans, and before He went to the cross.

Our prayers become the conduit through which God's power is released on earth. It is a mystery that I will never fully comprehend. God certainly does not have to wait for us to pray, but sometimes He chooses to do so.

We see in the Bible miraculous glory moments that follow times of extended prayer. Joshua prayed time would stop, and the "sun stood still" (Joshua 10:13). Daniel prayed for deliverance, and the lions went on a hunger strike (Daniel 6:22). Hannah prayed for a child, and her barren womb birthed a son (1 Samuel 1:20). Shadrach, Meshach, and Abednego prayed for safety, and they walked about in the fiery furnace unsinged (Daniel 3:26–27). Glory moments all!

Perhaps you read those verses and think, *Yes, that was then. This is now. That was them. This is me.*

But when you look closely at those men and women who experienced a sudden glory through prayer, you'll see that they were people just like you and me. I love James's description of Elijah and his amazing prayer: "Elijah was a man *just like us.* He prayed earnestly that it would not rain, and it did not rain on the land for three and a half years. Again he prayed, and the heavens gave rain, and the earth produced its crops" (James 5:17–18). For far too long I focused on the miracle of what Elijah did and missed the miracle of who he was. Elijah was a man "just like us." It was a moment of sudden glory when I realized that God put those three little words in that verse for men and women "just like us."

Oh, friend. God longs to commune with you through prayer. Yes, talk to Him. And then, listen. Sometimes He may simply want to tell you just how much He loves you. Other times He may give you instructions or reveal a profound truth. Either way, extended times of prayer can be the conduit through which glory moments flow.

Sudden Glory Moments Through Circumstances

God speaks through the Bible, through the Holy Spirit, through prayer, and He also speaks to us through various circumstances: a broken-down car, a sick child, a birthday celebration, a failure, a success, or a miraculous recovery. When union with God is your way of life, every circumstance carries within it the potential to become a glory moment with God. "The key is not the occurrence itself but the presence of the Holy Spirit as he communicates through life events. This does not mean we should seek a hidden meaning behind every traffic jam or thunderstorm. It does mean we should be sensitive to what God might be saying during the course of events in our day."[21]

Sometimes God speaks so eloquently through a life circumstance, you have no doubt that it was Him. You may be going through your day concentrating on the tasks at hand, and then when you least expect it, God speaks to you through a circumstance that catches you off guard and takes your breath away. Sometimes it is a sweet reminder of His presence, and other times it is the sting of stern conviction. I think a stern conviction is what the prophet Isaiah meant when he said, "The LORD spoke to me with his strong hand upon me" (Isaiah 8:11). Ouch.

One crisp December morning I was taking my son to school for a teacher conference. I don't know which had the greater chill—the morning air at six thirty or the tension between my son and me. Steven and I were not speaking. Just a few months before, he had transferred from a small Christian school of 489 students to a large public school of 2,500. While his social life was thriving in the new and exciting environment filled with diversity, diversion, and distractions, his grades were on the decline. Our drives to school were usually rather chatty, but not today. I was tired from worry. I was disappointed in his performance. I was frustrated.

We had already met with the Advanced Placement chemistry and English teachers. Today it was Mrs. Morris in Spanish 3. As we pulled up to the visitors' parking lot, the security guard stopped me.

"Sorry, ma'am," he said. "You can't park in this lot in the mornings."

"But this is where I was told to park. I have an appointment with a teacher," I explained.

"Well, this is where the buses for the handicapped kids unload in the mornings. I'll let you park in here today, but from now on, drive around to the other side of the school."

"Thanks," I said as I rolled my window back up. "I like this school less and less," I grumbled.

Steven just cut his eyes over my way as if to say, "Oh brother."

We met with Mrs. Morris. We played with numbers, and she offered suggestions on how to pull his grade up. I guess I was supposed to feel encouraged, but I didn't.

When I went back out to my car, the previously sleeping school was now bustling with activity. Buses filed in from every direction like ants on melted ice cream. Kids dressed in baggy jeans and clunky shoes with gargantuan backpacks slung over their shoulders brushed past me, rushing to make their first period class. The cold air slapped me in the face as I exited the building. I slid into my car, turned on the ignition, and backed out of my parking space. As I headed toward the exit, the same security guard blew his whistle and held up his hand for me to stop.

"What does he want now?" I huffed.

I turned my head to the left and discovered the reason for my delay. A bus filled with physically challenged teens was unloading. All I could do was wait—and watch. One boy caught my attention.

He was about fifteen years old, I guess. It was hard to tell because of the frailness of his frame. He wore thick glasses, a worn, tattered jacket, and a woolen cap on his head. His limbs twitched spasmodically as he tried to propel his body forward, and he clung to the doors of the bus in an attempt to steady his steps.

Three sunny adults waited to greet him and welcome him to another day of life. One woman held his arms to guide him down the two steps. Another simultaneously placed a helmet on his head and fastened the strap under his chin. A third woman held a walker steady until he could get a firm grasp on the cold steel handles. Then he grinned at the threesome, proud of his accomplishment.

At that moment, God spoke to my heart, *Sharon, look at those teachers' faces. What do you see?*

They are smiling, Lord.

Look at that boy's face. What do you see?

He's smiling, Lord.

Now, My child, look at your face in the mirror. What do you see?

The security guard walked over to my car and thumped on the hood to startle me out of my daze. "You can go now, ma'am."

I pulled out of the parking lot, barely able to drive because of the tears blurring my vision. For six weeks I had been unhappy because of my son's poor performance in school. And then God sent one of His precious children to remind me of the many blessings I had taken for granted.

When my husband came from work, he asked, "How was the teacher conference?"

"Oh, it was fine," I said, smiling happily. "But let me tell you about the one I had with God in the parking lot.

A sudden glory.

See, not all instances of sudden glory are warm and fuzzy. Some are painful…convicting…but love notes just the same.

SUDDEN GLORY MOMENTS THROUGH CREATION

Throughout the New Testament Jesus spoke in parables—illustrations to explain spiritual principles in terms the multitudes could understand. Jesus said that the kingdom of heaven is like a mustard seed, like a treasure hidden in a field, like a man who sowed good seed, like a net that was let down into the lake and caught all kinds of fish (see Matthew 13:31, 44, 24, 47). God still speaks through nature, proclaiming some of His most spectacular displays of glory. The whole earth is radiantly alive with His presence.

God longs for us to savor His majestic beauty and recognize His presence throughout creation. Paul wrote to the Romans, "Since the creation of the world God's invisible qualities—his eternal power and divine nature—have been clearly seen, being understood from what has been made, so that men are without excuse" (Romans 1:20). Just as God spoke to me of His love in the beautiful sunrise when He made His face shine upon me, He speaks eloquently and articulately through nature all around.

As Ann Voskamp says, "The weight of God's glory…daily and everywhere, punctures earth's lid and heaven falls through the holes."[22] The beauty of nature sparks romance, and we are the bride pursued once again. Every time you sense God speaking to you through creation, do not let your attention be arrested by the beauty alone, but allow the beauty to draw you into a clearer understanding of God's infinite glory that you will one day see without the confines of this world.

If we do not hear from God today, if we do not see His fingerprints through creation, we are without excuse. As we *live and move and have our being in Him,* we must, oh, we must turn aside and see God's glory in the vastness of the heavenlies and the minuteness of a flea. As Annie Dillard observed, "The world is fairly studded and strewn with unwrapped gifts and free surprises…cast broadside from a generous hand."[23]

"The whole earth is full of his glory" (Isaiah 6:3). God's lavish response to our longing for something more surrounds us, if we will but turn aside and see.

SUDDEN GLORY MOMENTS THROUGH PEOPLE

Have you ever received a word of encouragement from a stranger? a word of caution from a friend? a word of enlightenment from a child? Those words could very well have been God's words spoken to you through one of His messengers. And who knows, perhaps you have been one of God's messengers to someone else.

Paul referred to believers as "letters" from Christ, written not with ink but with the Spirit of the living God, not on tablets of stone but on tablets of human hearts (see 2 Corinthians 3:3). I have received many such letters over the years. No, they didn't have an envelope with a stamp in the right-hand corner or a return address in the left, but I knew exactly who sent them. One letter wore jeans and a sweatshirt, another a blue-and-white-striped dress. One letter wore teal capri pants, and another a girl's size 6X. All were God's letters sent to me in the form of His image bearers, reflecting His glory to a needy soul. Admittedly, some of God's letters had become marred in transit, and I suspect a few of the words were not quite what the Author intended. But they were His letters nonetheless.

Some of the letters I have received have been so beautifully scripted that I take them out and read them over and over again. They are treasures I hold dear.

One day I was walking through the grocery store when a Hispanic woman walked up to me, placed her hand on my arm, and looked me in the eye. "Jesus love you," she said in broken English.

"Thank you very much," I smiled with tears welling in my eyes.

How did she know that I needed that word of encouragement at that very moment? How *did* she know?

I suspect God prompted her heart to speak, and she spoke. As she *lived and moved and had her being in Christ,* He pointed her in my direction to deliver a much-needed word.

As you *live and move and have your being in Him,* listen closely; He may be prompting you to be a letter to someone who crosses your path. Don't miss it. You may be someone's love note from God. You may be the deliverer of a sudden glory.

God's Articulate Presence

I love, absolutely love, studying God's Word. From the time I first said yes to Jesus, I have devoured the Scriptures. And yet, I'll admit, extended times of prayer have been a struggle for me. Perhaps that is one reason it is called a discipline. I have to *discipline* myself to set the time apart—to "be still and know."

But one day I realized just how compartmentalized my time with God had become. My spiritual life was more like an outlined lesson plan with subheadings A, B, C, and 1, 2, 3 than a love relationship with Jesus. So I made a change. It was God's suggestion really. Why not pray and read at the same time?

When I read the Bible, I pray that the Holy Spirit will reveal what the words say, what they mean, and how I can apply them to my life. For example, one day while reading Ephesians 1:18, I felt compelled to pray this verse for several people. So I stopped reading and began communing with God in prayer.

Dear Lord, I pray for Steven today. I pray that You will open the eyes of his heart so that he may see the hope to which You have called him and the riches of his glorious inheritance in the saints... I prayed that scripture for several people, until I felt the promptings from the Holy Spirit cease. Then God and I got back to reading again.

Another day, I was reading Matthew 6:9, what we've come to know as the Lord's Prayer. "Our Father," Jesus began. *Stop right there and think about that,* the Holy Spirit seemed to say. *Our Father.* As I ruminated and marinated in the words *our* and *Father,* God spoke to my heart about the sort of father I'd always longed for and the sort of Father I already had in Him. If I had stuck to a schedule for my Bible reading that week, I would have fallen terribly behind. But the continual conversation I had with God about that one little word, *Father,* was priceless.

Consider the word *meditate.* This word often conjures up images of Eastern religious practices. But it is a wonderful word that we should not be afraid to use. *Meditation* simply means to think deeply and continuously about something. For a Christian, meditation and constant communication go hand in hand. As we think deeply and continuously about God's Word, He opens our eyes to see, our ears to hear, and our minds to understand. When you meditate on

Scripture, you mull over God's words in your mind until they move from your head to your heart.

Several years ago, a new game appeared in our Sunday newspapers and on bookstore shelves. It was called the Magic Eye. To the casual observer, a large colorful picture on a page looked like nothing more than an abstract of dots and squiggles. But if you stared at the picture just right, a beautiful three-dimensional image emerged. You would often hear someone shout, "I see it! I see it!" when the picture came into view.

That is the way of meditation. The dots and squiggles of God's Word become clear, and the reader shouts, "I see it! I see it!" A sudden glory.

Often, for me, the revelations of God's truth come into clear view as I go about my daily routine. I read a Scripture passage—communing with the Creator of the universe in the comfort of my own home (which is an astounding idea). The Holy Spirit illuminates my mind to focus on what God wants me to see. I chat with God about what the passage means and how I can apply it to my life. Then He sends me on holy field trips as I go about my day. I don't know that I'm going on a field trip, mind you, but it is a field trip nonetheless. For when we practice *in Him we live and move and have our being,* all of life is a field trip in which we see His principles put into practice in the physical realm.

God often gives us examples of scriptural principles through the dots and squiggles of life. And often, a beautiful picture comes into view as the Holy Spirit adjusts the lens so we can see clearly. Sometimes that happens the very day I read a particular scripture. Other times it may be weeks or months before I understand. But the key is to pay attention and not miss it. God will speak to you as one speaks to a dear friend.

Don't Miss It

If you had been among the 1,097 morning commuters bustling through Washington DC's Metro station at L'Enfant Plaza on January 12, 2007, you could have experienced an extraordinary gift. Tucked among the shoeshine vendors, newspaper kiosks, and lottery ticket dispensers, a young white man in jeans, long-sleeved T-shirt, and Washington Nationals baseball cap positioned himself against the wall beside a trash can. From a small case, he removed a violin. He left the open case at his feet and threw some spare change into it. Then he turned toward the huddled masses of rush-hour commuters and began to play. If you had been one of the seven who paused during their mad dash to work, you would have had a front row seat to Joshua Bell playing six of Bach's most difficult and exquisite violin pieces on a $3.5 million, three-hundred-year-old Stradivarius...for free.

It was an experiment by Gene Weingarten of the *Washington Post.* Joshua Bell, a concert violinist who normally earns a thousand dollars a minute, agreed to participate. As each commuter passed by, he or she had a decision to make. "Do I have time for beauty? Do I have time to pause, turn aside, and listen?"[24]

The fiddler standing against the bare wall at the top of the escalator was one of the finest classical musicians in the world, playing some of the most elegant music ever written on one of the most valuable violins ever made. And 1,090 busy men and women missed the gift because they were in a hurry.

Every day we have a choice. As we make Acts 17:28 a practical and perpetual reality in our lives, we will have a choice. We can rush through the day and miss God's magnificent displays of glory and articulate words of love, or we can turn aside and savor the incredible gift.

As we go through life, there comes a whisper, a faint call, a luring pull to a richer life which we sense we're passing by. Outer hurriedness and inner uneasiness are laced with hints that there is something more, something better, something that we're missing in the blur of life. "What could it be?" we ask.

When we embrace true union and abide in Christ, continual conversation becomes a way of life. All through the Bible we see that God spoke in various ways through various means. He spoke through dreams and visions, through a burning bush and a fiery mountain, through a donkey and an angel. He spoke by writing on a wall, by a wet fleece on the ground, and by forcing an almond branch into bloom. The important thing is not *how* God spoke but *that* He spoke. Equally important is for us to remember not *how* He will speak but *that He will* speak. And each one of the gentle whispers or startling shouts from God's heart to your heart carries within it the potential for moments of sudden glory. The key is not to miss them.

I have given you some broad categories and specific examples of how God reveals Himself and His glory to the human heart, but don't limit Him or box Him in. God never has been one to stick to a predictable pattern. He has no standard operating procedure when it comes to dealing with the human soul. He's infinitely creative and gloriously unpredictable. When you allow the Holy Spirit to sensitize your spirit, you will experience entirely new dimensions in your sacred relationship.

I pray Jacob's words will never come from my mouth or from yours: "Surely the LORD is in this place, and I was not aware of it" (Genesis 28:16). Instead, let's listen in expectation with the words of Isaiah on our lips: "He wakens me morning by morning, wakens my ear to listen like one being taught" (Isaiah 50:4).

His lavish response to our longing for something more awaits those who anticipate glory moments and awake in expectation.

5

DARING TO RAISE
YOUR EXPECTATIONS

> Disturb us, Lord…when our dreams have
> come true because we have dreamed too
> little.
>
> —SIR FRANCIS DRAKE, 1577

*W*hen I was in my early twenties, I did not have great
expectations for what my marriage would be like, if I
ever walked the aisle at all. My parents had a tumultuous relationship
from my earliest remembrance. Cycles of heated arguments and physical violence followed by silence and passive aggression were as predictable as the seasons. The atmosphere in our home was tense. It was
as if I lived on an earthquake fault line, never knowing when the "big
one" was going to hit. There were many "big ones."

I became a Christian when I was fourteen and resolved that if I ever got married, it would be to a man who loved Jesus with all his heart. Through the years, I dated many Christian young men. In my young mind, most of them were not very much fun.

So I had a conversation with God that went something like this: "Okay, God, if I ever get married, it will be to a Christian man. I'm committed to that. I won't give a guy a second glance unless he is a man who loves You with all his heart. It is not enough for him to *say* that he is a Christian. I want to see it in the way he lives his life, the way he uses his words, and the way he relates to other people. I'm going to pay attention to what he laughs at, what he watches on television, and how he handles anger. I know what I'm asking here. I know what I'm getting into. I realize that I most likely won't feel very passionate about this guy. I know that my life will probably be rather dull, boring, and lackluster. But that's okay. I'm holding out for a Christian man, no matter how humdrum and ho-hum he may be. If I like him pretty well, that's enough for me."

Oh my goodness! Talk about low expectations! I'm sure God got a big kick out of my request.

Here's what happened several years after that "prayer." When I was twenty-two, I returned to college to further my education. A young man from my hometown had a Bible study at his apartment and invited me to attend…and you'll remember this from chapter 2… When I walked in, I saw a young dental student sitting cross-legged on the floor and leaning up against the wall. His dark chocolate eyes looked up at me as he said, "Hi." I melted in a puddle.

After a few weeks, Steve finally asked me out on a date. But the venue of our rendezvous confirmed what I had expected all along.

"There is a missionary from Jackson, Mississippi, speaking over at

Murphy Hall," he explained. "I'd like to go hear him. Would you like to go with me?"

Well that certainly lined up with my expectations! Steve was handsome; no doubt about that. He was a Christian; that was for sure. But going to hear a missionary on our first date? He was going to be boring after all. But hey, what did I expect? (Now remember, I was young. I love missionaries! I am one! Just keeping it real.)

When he came to pick me up for our date, I wasn't quite ready. My apartment-mate welcomed him and directed him to the sofa to wait. While he perused the scattered magazines on the coffee table, some of my favorite music played on the stereo. In the South, we call it beach music. It's a type of sixties R&B Motown music.

When I finally emerged from my primping, Steve looked up and asked, "Do you like that kind of music?"

"Sure do," I replied. (I must say, I said it with an attitude of "and you gotta problem with that?")

"I do too," Steve said. "I have an entire collection. Do you know how to shag?" (That's a traditional Southern dance similar to a slow version of the swing.)

"I've been dancing the shag since I was in the fifth grade," I said.

"Let's see if we do it the same way," he said as he grabbed my hand.

I think I heard God laugh.

For twenty minutes we separated and came together as if we had been dancing together all our lives. He held my hand up and I spun under. He pulled me in and then rolled me out like a scroll. His shuffle kick mirrored my own.

You know what? We did go and hear the missionary on that crisp fall night in 1979. And afterward, we went to a favorite college hangout on the campus of UNC, the University of North Carolina at Chapel Hill, and danced until the doors closed. We had fun, and we haven't stopped having fun since. We have grown in God's grace, and we've graced the dance floor. Steve is the most *funnest* guy I have ever known, and he loves the Lord with all his heart. And to think I actually was ready to settle for just a nice Christian guy. God exceeded my expectations beyond all I ever could have asked or imagined.

But this isn't just about my love story with Steve. It is about my love story with Jesus. It is about yours too. And like my silly twenty-something prayer for a mediocre-but-nice husband, I fear we have lowered our expectations in our relationship with Jesus. He longs for an intimacy with us that ushers in a deep abiding joy, but I'm afraid we've settled for simply nice.

C. S. Lewis says that our lives should be filled with "merriment."[25] I like that word. *Merriment.* Just moving the words across my lips is fun. And I think Lewis is right. We lack merriment and we don't expect it. Many Christians look like they've been weaned on a dill pickle. My goodness, if there is anyone who should exude merriment, it is a person who knows Jesus as Savior and Lord. We, above all people, have something to be merry about!

What God desires, not *from* you but *for* you, is life to the full (John 10:10). There's nothing ho-hum about that. I read Jesus's words in John 10:10, and I am famished for glory moments of life to the full. I want to see God, to experience His presence as I *live and move and have my being in Him.*

John wrote, "How great is the love the Father has *lavished* on us, that we should be called children of God!" (1 John 3:1). He didn't simply use the word *given,* but *lavished.* Webster's dictionary defines *lavish* this way: "given or provided with great generosity and abundance, to bestow with large generosity, profusion, a downpour." Ponder those words separately.

Lavished.

Provided with great generosity.

Abundance.

Bestow with large generosity.

Profusion.

Downpour.

Do these words reflect your expectations in your relationship with Jesus? C. S. Lewis said it well:

> We are half-hearted creatures, fooling about with drink and sex
> and ambition when infinite joy is offered us, like an ignorant
> child who wants to go on making mud pies in a slum because
> he cannot imagine what is meant by the offer of a holiday at
> the sea. We are far too easily pleased.[26]

The first statement in the Westminster Shorter Catechism declares that man's chief end is to glorify God and enjoy Him forever. Enjoy Him! To enjoy God is to glorify Him. Just as He takes delight in you, He longs for you to take delight in Him. You simply can't separate the two.

Are you enjoying God? As you *live and move and have your being in Him,* is there a smile on your face and a skip in your step? Do you expect the rich adventurous faith-filled life that you read about in the Bible? Do you expect to experience God's glory today? If not, perhaps you need to raise your expectations of what your relationship with Jesus can be.

Once we've tasted the sweetness of His fruit, to settle for anything less than the bountiful orchard of His blessings will always disappoint. Oh yes, there are heavy-laden branches filled with low-hanging fruit just waiting to be picked. If only we would reach up high enough, raise our expectations, and pluck them from the tree.

Raising Our Expectations

While I came into the dating world with very low expectations for a future husband, I suspect—no, I take that back—I *know* many women come into marriage with *great* expectations. They expect their knight in shining armor to sweep them off their feet and to keep them off their feet. But for most, the shine on that armor begins to tarnish before the honeymoon pictures are secured in the photo album. Before you know it, romance becomes routine, matrimonial bliss morphs into mundane busyness, desire dwindles to duty, and passionate lovemaking becomes preplanned sex. After pouting and moping about the new state of affairs, with little effect on the bewildered husband I might add, most wives simply lower their expectations. And honestly, some of that may be good. Even a good husband makes a poor God. A man was never meant to meet a woman's every need…but Jesus is.

After a few years in the faith, many Christians lower their expectations of what their spiritual relationship with Jesus can be. When life doesn't turn out like one hopes, women often put up barriers to protect their hearts from being hurt again. Like lovers who have been wronged, many guard their hearts against future disappointment by lowering their expectations and asking for very little. Many throw themselves into predictable and controllable religious practices and neglect the relationship with Jesus. Relationship becomes religion, worship becomes work, and love becomes law. Some put God on the shelf in a tidy box and walk away. Clara did.

Dear Sharon:

I got married when I was thirty years old and was blessed with two children. My son and daughter are now twenty-two and twenty-one years old. I lost one child through late-term miscarriage. My husband was a pastor and then a Christian therapist. He died of brain cancer after we had been married seven years. I was a young widow left to raise our children, ages five and four. I've worked like a dog to provide for my kids. Who can measure and quantify their loss of a father or my loss of a mate? God takes away, and I stopped believing a long time ago that He will restore. The pain and loss are like smoldering embers in my heart. I find nothing but brokenness everywhere, like scattered shards of glass. A few years ago, I was diagnosed with bipolar II and have had to deal with that without a support system. I know about grief and I know about pain.

My life before marriage was also impacted with loss. My mom suffered with psychosis all her life and had a complete emotional breakdown when I was in sixth grade. My father died of a heart attack suddenly when I was nineteen. I am a broken person that God can do nothing with. I rarely ask God for anything anymore.

—Clara

Clara's e-mail, like so many others filled with tragedy, hit me in the gut. Broken dreams, shattered lives, and no hope for better times. And yet, as I read the words, "I rarely ask God for anything anymore," I sensed a spark of hope imbedded in the ink—a secret code for the discerning sleuth. *Clara wrote to me.*

God had not walked away from Clara. I have no idea why she has experienced so much pain in her life, but I do know that God doesn't want her to pull up the covers and call it quits. The mere fact that she had the courage to hit Send on her e-mail shows that she has a niggling hope that there could be something better. Maybe the hope that, *Perhaps I've misunderstood.* God tells me to pray for her. And I do. While she may not have the strength to ask God for anything anymore, I can ask Him for her.

Clara called out to God in her own way, but she must, oh, she must open her eyes to see God reaching out to her. We can pray and still not expect God to answer.

In the early years of the church, King Herod had many Christians murdered and many more put in prison. James, the brother of John, was put to death with the sword, and Peter was thrown into prison.

The night before Peter was to be taken to trial, a group gathered at the house of Mary (John's mother) to pray for him. While they were praying, there was a knock at the door. A servant girl named Rhoda answered it.

"Who's there?" she asked.

"It's Peter," the freed apostle answered.

She knew it was Peter—she recognized his voice! God had answered their prayers! Rhoda was so excited, she didn't even let Peter in but ran back to tell the group that he was standing at the door.

Makes me smile!

"You're out of your mind," they told her. "Maybe it's his angel."

Peter kept knocking. Finally they opened the door and were astonished to see Peter, alive and well, standing right in front of them. (See Acts 12.)

Why were they surprised? Why didn't they believe Rhoda? While they were praying for Peter's release, they didn't really expect God to free him. Do you see it? We can pray about a situation and miss the glory moment knocking at the door because of unbelief and low expectations that God would actually answer.

Sometimes I fear we have lowered our spiritual expectations to match the experiences of people we know rather than what we read in the Bible. We look around and see what has occurred in the lives of other believers, and that's where we set the bar. As a result, we lead mediocre lives, forfeiting the abundant life Jesus came to give.

Bob told me about a visit to Vietnam, where he met with a leader of an underground Christian church. This leader, who had spent a large part of his life in prison for his faith, told Bob many stories of the growth of Christians, as approximately one million believers met in hidden huddles all around the country. "What everybody wants is to see God move," the pastor explained.

And isn't that the desire of your heart—to see God move in your life and also in the lives of those you love? Jesus reminds us, "My Father is always at his work to this very day, and I, too, am working" (John 5:17). Always at His work. Always. And yet, do you expect to see it? Are you willing, along with me, to raise your expectations and anticipate seeing God's glory through His work in your life today? Are you willing to raise your expectations to experience moments of sudden glory?

I sat in a Sunday school room with a group of fellow baby boomers as Bob shared about his experience with this Vietnamese pastor. And at the close of the lesson, Bob opened up the floor for the class members to tell of a time when they experienced God moving in their lives.

"When I was sixteen…," one began.

"When I was twenty-seven…," another chimed in.

"Several years ago…," still another shared.

I was struck. We should have all been waving our hands and excited to begin with these words: "Yesterday God showed me…" "This morning God revealed to me…"

Why do we have to go so far back into the archives of our lives to look for that one time we recognized God moving in our lives? I dare say that we miss the glory moments that flash before us and even linger around us because we don't expect them to be there.

I want to challenge you to make a list. Get a notebook or a journal and write "A Sudden Glory" across the top. Then begin chronicling how God makes Himself known to you today…and tomorrow…and the next day. We've provided a few pages in the back of this book for you to begin…just to begin. I am sure you will have far more to record than this small space would allow, but I don't want you to wait another minute to get started!

David wrote:

I will exalt you, my God the King;
    I will praise your name for ever and ever.
Every day I will praise you
    and extol your name for ever and ever.

> Great is the LORD and most worthy of praise;
>> his greatness no one can fathom.
> One generation will commend your works to another;
>> they will tell of your mighty acts.
> They will speak of the glorious splendor of your majesty,
>> and I will meditate on your wonderful works.
> They will tell of the power of your awesome works,
>> and I will proclaim your great deeds.
> They will celebrate your abundant goodness
>> and joyfully sing of your righteousness. (Psalm 145:1–7)

That's one party I don't want to miss! David recognized what God was doing in his own life. He listened to what God was doing in other people's lives. And then he invited all to join together and tell about the glory moments in a grand celebration. Merriment at its best. "Let the redeemed of the LORD tell their story" (Psalm 107:2).

READING SCRIPTURE WITH FRESH EYES

Several years ago I went on a missions trip to the West Indies. Part of our mission included distributing reading glasses to the islanders. I'll never forget handing a Bible to a leathery-faced, elderly man.

"Can you read this?" I asked as I pointed to a psalm.

In polished Old English, he began, "The LORD is my shepherd; I shall not want..." I listened as he delivered a well-rehearsed Psalm 23 in perfect King James. The problem was, it was not a King James Version of the Bible; it was the Living Bible. He was not reading the words. He was quoting them from memory.

We tried on various reading glasses, chose a pair suitable for him, and then I handed him the Bible again. "Let's try that again," I smiled. "Read this for me."

He looked at the pages and a grin spread across his crinkled mahogany face. "Because the Lord is my Shepherd, I have everything I need!" This time he read the words.

That's why I read the Bible in different translations. I can grow so accustomed to the words on the page that I miss the meaning in my heart. Various translations keep me from glossing over the words carelessly.

Suppose we, like my island friend, read God's letter to us with fresh eyes, and just suppose we believed Him. What would that do to our not-so-great expectations?

Consider this: "Because we approach the gospel with preconceived notions of what it should say rather than what it does say, the Word no longer falls like rain on the parched ground of our souls. It no longer sweeps like a wild storm into the corners of our comfortable piety. It no longer vibrates like sharp lightning in the dark recesses of our nonhistoric orthodoxy. The gospel becomes, in the words of Gertrude Stein, 'a pattering of pious platitudes spoken by a Jewish carpenter in the distant past.'"[27]

Do you want to raise the bar on your spiritual expectations? Do you dare? Then read the Bible with fresh eyes—and believe it. "Oh, I believe it," most Christians would say. But let me give you just one example. Jesus said: "I tell you the truth, anyone who has faith in me will do what I have been doing. He will do even greater things than these, because I am going to the Father" (John 14:12).

Do you believe that? Do I? It is startling. I even feel uncomfortable reading the words out loud. Why do I have an easier time believing the words are for someone else rather than for me?

When we base our expectations on God's Word rather than what we see happening in the spiritual lives of others, they grow pregnant with possibilities.

"But God doesn't work today like He did back in biblical times," some argue. Who says He doesn't? Don't tell the folks in Nigeria who have seen countless blind receive their sight. Don't tell the folks in the underground church in China that God doesn't rattle jail cells and set captives free. Don't tell that to the little boy who walked out of the hospital cancer free with no medical explanation for the cure. Don't tell that to the thousands of people who have *not* had their great expectations of God civilized and educated right out of them and who experience miraculous glory moments in the mundane on a regular basis.

But isn't it risky to believe everything the Bible says is true for us today? Yes, it is. So what is the alternative? Do we lower our expectations of God to protect ourselves from disappointment? Expect little. Receive little.

> It is one thing to believe God could perform a miracle in the
> Bible, or a thousand years ago, or even in the life of a friend; it
> is quite another matter to wholeheartedly believe God can do
> anything He chooses to do in our lives![28]

Paul wrote: "No eye has seen, no ear has heard, no mind has conceived what God has prepared for those who love him" (1 Corinthians 2:9). As we *live and move and have our being* in Christ, we will experience sudden glories if we expect God to do what He said He would do, for the atmosphere of expectation becomes the breeding ground for moments of sudden glory to manifest in the miraculous and mundane.

Abundance is at the very heart of the great I AM. We can come to Him in joyful expectation of receiving all we need…and sometimes more. When we believe God is who He says He is and that He will do what He says He will do, Ephesians 3:20–21 becomes our reality: "Now to him who is able to do immeasurably more than all we ask or imagine, according to his power that is at work within us, to him be *glory* in the church and in Christ Jesus throughout all generations, for ever and ever! Amen."

God longs for you to live in joyful union with Him as you taste and see that He is good and to warm at knowing that you have captured His heart. I am my Beloved's and He is mine.

I cry out with Sir Francis Drake:

Disturb us, Lord, when
We are too well pleased with ourselves,
When our dreams have come true
Because we dreamed too little,
When we arrived safely
Because we sailed too close to the shore.

Disturb us, Lord, when
With the abundance of things we possess,
We have lost our thirst
For the waters of life;
Having fallen in love with life,

We have ceased to dream of eternity
And in our efforts to build a new earth,
We have allowed our vision
Of the new Heaven to dim.

Disturb us, Lord, to dare more boldly,
To venture on wider seas
Where storms will show your mastery;
Where losing sight of land,
We shall find the stars.

We ask you to push back
The horizons of our hopes;
And to push into the future
In strength, courage, hope, and love.[29]

Disturb us, Lord.

BELIEVING GOD

It doesn't take reading very far into the Bible to see the weighty importance of believing God. Abraham believed God, and it was credited to him as righteousness (Genesis 15:6). His wife, Sarah, had a much harder time believing that God could fulfill His promises. The angel asked her, "Is anything too hard for the LORD?" (Genesis 18:14). That is a question each and every one of us will have to answer at one time or another.

In the Greek, the original language of the New Testament, the word *pistis* is translated as "faith," "believing," and "believe." The noun *pistis* and the verb form of the same word, *pisteuo* occur more than 240 times in the New Testament, and the adjective *pistos* is found sixty-seven times.[30] That's a lot of believing God!

When the Philippian jailer asked, "Sirs, what must I do to be saved?" Paul and Silas answered without hesitation, "*Believe* in the Lord Jesus, and you will be saved" (Acts 16:30–31). It is *whoever believes in him* that does not perish but has everlasting life (John 3:16). Paul wrote to the Ephesians:

> And you also were included in Christ when you heard the word
> of truth, the gospel of your salvation. Having *believed,* you were
> marked in him with a seal, the promised Holy Spirit, who is
> a deposit guaranteeing our inheritance until the redemption
> of those who are God's possession—to the praise of his glory.
> (Ephesians 1:13–14)

When you believed in Jesus, you were signed, sealed, delivered—you're His! It is a decision that every Christian has made in the past. And with that decision comes forgiveness of sins and everlasting life. Hallelujah!

Then there's more. Paul went on to pray:

> I pray also that the eyes of your heart may be enlightened in
> order that you may know the hope to which he has called you,
> the riches of his glorious inheritance in the saints, and his in-
> comparably great power for us who *believe.* That power is like
> the working of his mighty strength, which he exerted in Christ

when he raised him from the dead and seated him at his right
hand in the heavenly realms. (verses 18–20)

The word *pistis* in the first passage is past tense—*believed*. However *pistis* in the second passage is a present active participle, which
means we believe and we keep on believing, right now, all the time,
continuously. And what happens when we *believe* God tells the
truth? We will have access to His incomparably great power…"like
the working of his mighty strength, which he exerted in Christ when
he raised him from the dead and seated him at his right hand in the
heavenly realms." Now if that doesn't raise our expectations for this
faith journey of union and communion with Jesus, I don't know
what would!

Theresa believed God…and dared to trust God to answer her
child's prayer. Theresa's daughter always wanted to play the flute, but
it seemed financially impossible. "Honey, we can't afford a flute," she
explained. "Maybe one day."

The following year, her daughter once again expressed her desire
to join the school band and learn to play the flute. Theresa didn't
have the heart to tell her no again. "If it is God's will for you to
play the flute," she explained, "then He will provide one before the
school year starts. Let's ask Him to take care of it." Theresa prayed
and believed God would answer, but she had no idea how He would
provide.

A few days before school started, Theresa and her daughter went
to a yard sale. And what did they see glistening in the sunlight among
all the wares? A flute! But this wasn't just any ol' flute. This was an
antique flute that had Theresa's daughter's birthday inscribed on the

side. The year was 1918, but the day and month were the same as hers. A sudden glory!

The miracle flute was not a fluke. Theresa dared to ask, dared to believe, and God lavishly gave. Today Theresa's daughter plays the flute beautifully, and every time she brings the instrument to her lips, she remembers that moment of sudden glory glistening in the sunlight.

During Jesus's three-and-a-half years on earth, His miracles, messages, and ministry encouraged people to raise their expectations and experience God in new and fresh ways. The Bible bulges with promises that await all who believe. Jesus stirred listeners' hearts with words such as "Ask and it will be given to you; seek and you will find; knock and the door will be opened to you. For everyone who asks receives; he who seeks finds; and to him who knocks, the door will be opened" (Matthew 7:7–8).

One day, as Jesus walked down the road, a man born blind called out to Him.

"Jesus, Son of David, have mercy on me!"

"Shhh, be quiet" the crowd shushed.

"Jesus, Son of David, have mercy on me!" he cried out again.

Then Jesus stopped and asked the beggar, "What do you want Me to do for you?" (see Luke 18:35–40).

Every time I read those words, they catch my breath. *What do you want Me to do for you?* Would you dare believe that Jesus would ask you the same question? I believe He already has.

I sit with the blind beggar—face upturned, cupped hands raised. "Lord, I want to see" (verse 41). For it is in the seeing that I will experience the moments of sudden glory that satisfy my ache for something more.

DESIRING HIS DESIRES

On another occasion, Jesus sought to raise the expectations of a used and abused woman from Samaria. After being tossed away by five different husbands, she was now living with a man who was not her husband. I suspect her expectations for marriage as well as for life were very low. So Jesus sat by a well, in the heat of the day, and waited for His God-given assignment to arrive.

When the lone woman came to the well, Jesus asked, "Will you give me a drink?" Oh, friend, Jesus did not need for that woman to give Him a drink. He had a purpose and a plan to give *her* one. A lengthy conversation ensued. As a matter-of-fact, it is the longest conversation between Jesus and any one person recorded in all four gospels. The turning point of the exchange occurred when Jesus made a statement to make her thirsty for more in life.

"If you knew the gift of God and who it is that asks you for a drink, you would have asked him and he would have given you living water" (John 4:10). Jesus salted her thirst with these words and then went on to pour living water on her parched heart with the news: He was the Messiah who had come to give her what she had been searching for her entire life—unfailing love.

I shout with my Samaritan friend, "Give me that water!" I hope you do too.

This encounter was never about what Jesus wanted *from* her— water from Jacob's well. It was all about what God wanted *for* her—a flow of living water to course through her soul as she *lived and moved and had her being in Him.* Jesus took a woman beaten down by life and raised her expectations to what the glory life could really be.

The gospel is more than a self-improvement plan. It is more than a way to get what you want when you want it. It is more than a savings bond to cash in at the end of your life. The gospel is a story of God's desire to reunite mankind back to Himself and make *in Him we live and move and have our being* a reality in your life. It is God's lavish response to your ache for something more.

The writer of Psalm 37:4 wrote: "Delight yourself in the LORD and he will give you the desires of your heart." Far too many Christians have read those words and hung their hats on a name-it-and-claim-it prosperity gospel, which is really no gospel at all. They've put the emphasis on the wrong word in the sentence. It is no surprise that we, in our self-centered society, have made the verse focus on ourselves rather than on God.

Let's read it again, putting the emphasis where it belongs—on God Himself. "Delight yourself in the LORD and *he* will give you the desires of your heart." When you cultivate your relationship with God, you begin to see life from *His* perspective and your desires begin to line up with *His* desires. His desires become your desires, and your prayers will elevate to a heavenly standard that asks for the very things God desires. What matters most to God will begin to matter most to you…and that is your relationship with Him. Always your intimate relationship.

Let's look at that word *delight*. The Hebrew word *hapes* refers to taking joy or pleasure in something or someone. It is synonymous with the verb "to love" and "to be pleased." At times, *hapes* denotes the action of seeking or desiring to do what will bring happiness, pleasure, fulfillment, or satisfaction. An English idiom that expresses this meaning of *hapes* is "to have one's heart set on someone or something."[31] He longs for your delight to be in Him, as His delight is in you. I think of Ephesians 1:4 yet again: "Long before he laid down earth's foundations, he had us in mind, had settled on us as the focus of his love, to be made whole and holy by his love" (MSG).

God longs for you to throw yourself into the river of His love. He desires for you to purpose in your heart and mind to drift along in the current of His perfect plan. When you do, whether careening on quiet streams or battling through violent rapids, you will know that wherever you go, it is *in Him you live and move and have your being.* No matter where the river of His will may lead, He is there protecting, guiding, and sustaining as you traverse the unpredictable waters of life. We can begin each day with the words, "This is the day the Lord has made," knowing that His abundant presence fills every bit of it.

When we raise our expectations of what our intimate relationship with Jesus can be, we will notice His outstretched hand inviting us to experience life in a whole new way. *In Him we live and move and have our being* becomes more than a walk, a march, or even a race. It becomes a beautiful dance uniquely choreographed by God just for you.

6

SAYING YES

TO GOD'S DIVINE DANCE

> Once the Lord has fed His child through
> intimate devotions, He begins to call him
> more pointedly to deeper obedience....
> Obedience for this individual is no longer
> a burden, undertaken only because the
> Bible tells him to do something. Rather,
> obedience becomes a joy because his closest
> friend and most compassionate Lord
> beckons him to be like Him.
> —BRUCE WILKINSON, *Set Apart*

*O*ver the course of several years, my husband and I trav-
eled many times to Sea Island, Georgia, and beheld art
in motion as seasoned couples graced the dance floor to the sounds

of a big band orchestra. Mirrored steps, swirling dresses, and graceful twosomes moved around the parquet in a kaleidoscope of colors. Watching them stirred up a hunger in me to learn how to do the same.

So Steve and I signed up for a six-week introductory ballroom dance class at a local studio.

"Steve and Sharon," the instructor began, "the first dance we will learn is the fox trot. Steve, extend your left arm. Now place your right hand on your wife's left shoulder blade. Cup it firmly in your hand. Let her know it's there." Then she turned to me, "Sharon, you gently rest your left hand on your husband's right shoulder and place your right hand into his left hand. Keep your backs straight. Taut. This is called your frame."

So far, so good.

She then proceeded to teach us to make little boxes with our feet while counting one, two, three, four, one, two, three, four. This was not floating around the dance floor like the couples on Sea Island. This was not what I had in mind.

The instructor continued teaching as we marched in place. "Steve, you have the hardest part because it is up to you to lead. All Sharon has to do is follow your signals. With a gentle press to her back, she will know to move forward. With a slight release, she will know to move backward. When you raise your arm, she will know to turn under."

Sounded easy enough, but it wasn't. More than once, the instructor tapped me on the shoulder and said, "Sharon, you're leading again." The problem was, when I led, Steve wouldn't follow. Imagine that. Now I know a train can't have two engines, but I felt I was the better dancer and the lessons would go much quicker if Steve would just let me lead. But my tendency to take control only slowed us down and frustrated the entire process.

After we mastered tiny boxes, it was time for lesson number two. "Okay," the instructor continued, "now you are ready to begin moving around the room. This will be like making small boxes with a flap open."

We learned how to take two steps forward and two steps to the side, two steps forward and two steps to the side. Actually, Steve got to move forward, but I had to move backward, which seemed very unfair to me. "I understand that we can't both move forward, but why am I the one who has to move backward?" I complained. The instructor took a deep breath and assured me that this was the way God planned it. (She didn't explain it exactly that way, but I knew that's what she meant.)

So the three of us marched and counted: "Slow, slow, quick, quick. Slow, slow, quick, quick." I felt more like a shopping buggy being pushed around the room than a dance partner, gliding with grace. I was just glad no one was watching.

I had wanted us to be the next Ginger Rogers and Fred Astaire, but instead we looked more like Fred Rogers and Mrs. Frog dancing about the neighborhood. And all during our six weeks of lessons, the instructor kept tapping me on the shoulder and saying, "Sharon, you're leading again."

Eventually, I did learn to trust Steve enough to let him lead. Did you catch that? I learned to *trust* him. As long as I didn't trust him, then I would never yield to his promptings. As long as I thought I could do it better, I would never follow his lead. But when I surrendered to his tender tugs and gentle releases, we began to glide. When I began to heed his cues, I knew when to spin, roll out like a casted fishing line, and be reeled back in again like a prized catch.

Amazingly, when I relinquished control and followed Steve's lead, I looked good. I was the one spinning, twirling, rolling out, and swirling back in. All Steve got to do was stay in one place and drive the machine.

And that is the joy and beauty of practicing a life of union with Jesus. *In Him we live and move and have our being* becomes a graceful dance in which we simply learn to follow Jesus's lead. When we learn to yield to Jesus's tender tugs and gentle releases, when we relinquish our tendency to take control, we move as one to the melody of heaven's big band and God's creative choreography designed uniquely for each of us. But there is always a choice.

THE MISCONCEPTION OF OBEDIENCE

When my son was two years old, his favorite word was *no.* "Steven, put up your toys," was met by, "No." "Steven, time for a nap," was countered with, "No." "Steven, eat your green beans," was resisted with, "No." (Lest you think *no* meant anything to me, it did not. I always won the battle of the wills with this pint-size lump of love God had given me.) One day he fell off of his little plastic three-wheeler and instead of crying, he stood up, placed his chubby hands on his determined hips, and yelled at his Hot Wheels, "No!" It was the worst word he could think of and, by golly, he was going to say it.

From the beginning of time we see that obedience to God has been a problem for all humanity. That word *no* seems to ride the wave of disobedience as the undertow of poor choices pulls us down. "I did it my way," the proud sing for all to hear.

Why is that? Oh sure, it's easy to say that it's due to our sin nature and our inherent desire to control. But what about after we come to Christ? Doesn't 2 Corinthians 5:17 say that we are a brand-new creation? Doesn't Galatians 2:20 say, "I have been crucified with Christ and I no longer live, but Christ lives in me"? Doesn't Scripture teach that our old nature that was rebellious toward God, separated from God, and antagonistic toward God has been replaced with a new nature that is reconciled or brought into oneness with God? Then why do we still struggle with obedience?

There are many reasons, but let me suggest just one. Could it be that we don't believe that God has our best interests in mind? Could it be that we see Him as a cruel taskmaster cracking the whip of submission over our backs rather than a loving Father who wants the best for His child? Could it be that we don't trust Him?

When I set up rules for my son, I didn't do it out of meanness. I wasn't out to ruin his fun. No, I set up boundaries in which he could flourish, so that he *could* flourish. God does the same with us. He sets up boundaries in which we can flourish, and when we step out of those parameters, we suffer the consequences. God's laws are not meant to restrict us but to protect us and provide a safe place for us to flourish. It is within those boundaries that the glory life exists.

Jesus knew we'd have trust issues when it came to obedience. "Which of you fathers, if your son asks for a fish, will give him a snake instead?" He asked. "Or if he asks for an egg, will give him a scorpion? If you then, though you are evil, know how to give good gifts to your children, how much more will your Father in heaven give the Holy Spirit to those who ask him!" (Luke 11:11–13).

If we don't understand that God always, *always* wants what is best for us, then we will have a difficult time trusting His lead. *In Him we live and move and have our being* will be a halted walk at best.

> If we continue to picture God as a small-minded bookkeeper,
> a niggling customs officer rifling through our moral suitcase, as
> a policeman with a club who is going to bat us over the head
> every time we stumble and fall, or as a whimsical, capricious,
> and cantankerous thief who delights in raining on our parade
> and stealing our joy, we flatly deny what John writes in his first
> letter (4:16): "God is love." In human beings, love is a quality, a
> high-prized virtue; in God, love is His identity.[32]

And it is because of that love that you can always trust that He has your best interest in mind.

When we truly believe that God always wants what's best for us, then we begin to understand that obedience is not something we *have* to do; rather, obedience is something we *get* to do.

Do you want to experience an adventurous, intimate relationship with Jesus in which you sense His presence? Do you want your in-loveness with God to grow to new heights and depths that you never thought possible? Then follow His lead. That's exactly where He wants to take you.

In my research I checked my concordance for verses on obedience. The word is mentioned in almost every book in the Bible, which says to me, "This is important." It is one of the key themes of the Bible. It is within the borders of the obedient life that moments of sudden glory abound as you *live and move and have your being in Him.*

The life of obedience is chock-full of glory moments. Not because He simply rewards you for good behavior, but because obedience to God is the door behind which the grand prize is hidden—the sweet life of union filled with intimate moments of sudden glory in which you know, oh you know, that He has pulled out all the stops to draw you into His embrace yet again.

We have looked at obedience far too long as what God wants *from* us rather than what God wants *for* us. That is worth saying again. God does not need our obedience. He has thousands of angels standing ready to do His bidding with but a word. *We* are the ones who need our obedience. When we turn a deaf ear to His still small voice, we forfeit fulfillment, miss miracles, and prevent promises from becoming our reality. The loss is ours...not His. We miss out on what God wants to do in and for us and even with us.

We can be like the rich young ruler who said, "No, thanks. My dance card is full." Or we can be like Jesus's eleven closest friends, who said, "Yes, Lord," and changed the world. Interestingly, the rich young ruler knew the Scriptures. He even had obeyed the ones Jesus quoted (see Matthew 19:16–22 and Luke 18:18–25). He was a religious man. But the words made very little difference in his life. We never heard from him again. God always gives us a choice.

SHALL WE DANCE?

Sometimes I look at my life today and wonder how in the world I got to this place of ministry. And then I realize that much of the reason I am here is because I chose to trust God's leading, even when, especially when, it didn't make any earthly sense at all. Then I wonder about all the missed opportunities because I didn't.

Many years ago I had a ministry opportunity that seemed way beyond my ability...and it was. I wasn't qualified. I wasn't trained. I didn't have a theology degree. I only took one English class in college—the one required to graduate.

Did you notice how many of those sentences in that last paragraph started with the word *I*? I certainly did. Just as surely as Paul filled Romans 7 with more *I*'s than any good writer should, I filled my mind with personal pronouns that shined the spotlight on my own insecurities and inadequacies rather than God's sufficiency.

For one year I had been praying that God would show me what my next phase of life was to look like. I was a wife, a mother, a dental hygienist, a Bible study teacher, a crisis pregnancy counselor, and a volunteer for a host of worthy causes. But my soul was restless.

I had created a few Bible studies for my home church, written a couple of articles for various magazines, and scribbled a file folder full of personal stories with spiritual applications. "God, do you want me to do something with all this writing?" I asked. Then I waited. And I waited. And I waited.

While strolling through a garden tour, a friend of mine mentioned a possibility. "There's a gal who is starting a new ministry in town. Maybe you should talk to her. I bet she could use some help." I wasn't looking for more to do, just that *one* thing to do. But I tucked that information in the little "wait and see" compartment of my mind and mulled over it for a few days.

Eventually I met with Lysa and she shared her vision for a ministry to encourage and equip families, especially wives and mothers. I agreed to record a few radio segments with her based on some of my stories. After we finished the session she turned to me and began, "For one year, I've been praying for a ministry partner. I think God is showing me that you are the one."

I didn't know the first thing about radio recording, production, or distribution. And yet, here was this young woman telling me that God had whispered into her ear that I was to be her partner in a new upstart ministry venture that included writing, speaking, and radio.

"Thank you for asking, Lysa," I replied. "But I think you've heard wrong. I don't know anything about radio. I just like to write stories. But I'll certainly pray about it."

We parted ways and I thought to myself, *That was crazy. What a silly idea. I don't know anything about radio. That's not something I could do.*

I told her I would pray about it, because that's what a nice Christian girl *would* say. But I had no intention of saying yes.

A few weeks later, Steve and I got up on Sunday morning, and the restlessness continued to play over my spirit. "Steve, let's go to a different church this morning. Just for fun. Let's go over to that big church that has the choir that sounds like the Brooklyn Tabernacle. I could really use some cutting-loose praise and worship today."

"Sounds good to me," Steve replied.

So off we went to a church that was not our own. When we arrived, we discovered that a visiting preacher, who was not their own, was slated to teach that day. After thirty minutes of incredible worship, the visiting pastor approached the podium. "Well, I had a sermon all prepared, but God has just changed it. Forget what's printed in your bulletin. I'm going to preach from John chapter 2 today."

So off he went down a road that God had paved. The pastor painted a picture of Jesus at the wedding of Cana with His mother and a few of His best friends. Leave it to Mary, Jesus's mother, to notice the party details. The wine was just about to run out, and the seven-day celebration was in full swing. For a host to run out of wine was a serious offense and a social embarrassment.

"Jesus," she whispered, "they are running out of wine."

"What's that to Me?" he replied.

With a twinkle in her eye, Mary turned to the wine stewards and said, "Whatever He says do, do it."

It was as if that pastor looked right at me in the sea of thousands. Whether or not he did, I don't know. But I do know God spoke directly to me. *Did you hear that, Sharon? Whatever I say do, do it.*

God had written those words on the heart of this man standing behind the podium, sealed them in an envelope of the sermon, and express mailed them to me. Fifth row, second seat. My name was on the envelope just as sure as if the pastor had called out my name. The postmark was clear. It was a sudden glory.

Yes, God had been stirring the pot of my life's soup. And now it was time to serve it up. But would I take His hand and join Him on the dance floor, or sit this one out because of fear?

I had to make a move. I had to decide. I had to choose to obey or not. Even though what I felt He was asking me to do made absolutely no sense at all, I had a choice. "Whatever He says do, do it." As I said before, we always have a choice.

TIMELY TWO-STEP

As we drove home that afternoon, I thought of Peter and John's fishing surprise. All night they had been on the open sea casting their ropes and hauling in empty nets. Other than algae, seaweed, and a few bits of trash, their nets had brought in nothing. No fish. No income. No food to feed the hungry mouths that depended on them back at home.

As the sun made its way over the horizon, the discouraged men washed their nets on the shore. Then Jesus, the carpenter and teacher, followed by a hungry crowd, asked to use their boat as a platform. He got into Peter's boat, pushed away from the shore a bit, and began to teach the crowds sitting along the beach. When he had finished teaching, He turned to Peter. "Put out into deep water, and let down the nets for a catch" (Luke 5:4).

I can just hear Peter now: "Good grief, John. Do you hear that guy? We've been fishing all night and caught nothing. Then here comes this country carpenter telling us how to do our job. He doesn't know the first thing about fishing. Real fishermen don't even fish during the daytime. We fish at night. We're the professionals here. But I'll be polite."

"Sir, we've fished all night and caught nothing. But because you say so, we'll do it" (see Luke 5:5).

Peter and John rowed away from the shore and hoisted the freshly cleaned nets one more time. Just then, the God of the universe, who created the fish and the seas, whistled for the schools of fish to head for the nets. The fish filled the nets like teenagers pouring into a rock concert.

Peter and John must have laughed. I would have. The catch was so large that the nets began to break. They couldn't even contain all the fish. Exceedingly abundantly more than they could have ever asked or imagined. Abundant. Lavish. Extravagant. A sudden glory!

Can you just imagine the size of their eyes, the drop of their jaws, the strain of their muscles as they pulled in the blessing? Not only were Peter and John blessed because of their obedience, they called their friends in to enjoy their bounty as well. Oh, the moments of sudden glory that fill our nets when we *live and move and have our being* in obedience to the One who loves us most.

"Because you say so…"

Notice what Peter did after he hauled in the miraculous catch. He left it all behind and followed Jesus to become a fisher of men. That was the real catch of the day. Oh, how silly we are to think that the true riches are simply financial gain. Peter had financial gain with this incredible catch, and yet he left it all behind to follow the God who pursued and caught his heart.

"Put out into deep water, and let down the nets for a catch." It was a simple request—nothing earth shattering. Peter had no idea that obeying Jesus would lead to such an all-encompassing, life-changing experience. Our little acts of obedience may do the same. Don't look for the seemingly big showy acts of obedience to get your name in heavenly lights. People might be impressed, but God won't be. Look for, listen for, and watch for the daily responses to His nudges—opportunities for sudden glory all.

As you accept Jesus's invitation onto the dance floor of obedience, don't be surprised if the simplest moves of the beginner grow more and more elaborate as you say yes to Him. As Steve and I practiced what we learned in those beginner dance classes, our steps became more and more complex. We're still no Fred and Ginger, but we have a few smooth moves and a bit of fancy footwork that we enjoy.

It's not necessarily what God wants you to do *for* Him; it's what He wants to do *for* you as you move *with* Him. As you practice Acts 17:28, become sensitive to God's promptings, and trust His lead, your steps will become stunningly beautiful and gloriously graceful.

Fancy Footwork

I remember complaining to the dance instructor, "How many times are we going to have to go over the one-two-three-four of the fox trot? I'm tired of making these little boxes. I want to move around the room! I want to dip and swirl!"

Then she reminded me, "As soon as you learn to follow your husband's lead and master the basic steps, we'll move on to fancier moves."

As you *live and move and have your being in Him,* the places He will lead you will become more and more glorious as you learn to relinquish control and trust Him. Small steps of obedience become beautiful sweeping moves of faith.

When people ask me how I got started in ministry, I tell them I started by writing for *free* publications for *free* for ten years. This is not what most people want to hear. When I tell them I started by folding newsletters in the den of my home for several years, they seem crestfallen. When I tell them I started out by cleaning the bathrooms in our first little ministry office, they seem confused.

"No, I mean how did you get started writing and speaking?" they ask.

"I'm telling you," I reply. "This is how I got started. Being faithful in the little things. By doing what God led me to do on any particular day."

We don't obey God in the seemingly small assignments in order to get the bigger ones. However, God will never entrust someone with a big assignment who has not proved herself trustworthy in the small.

When God invites you to the dance floor, what you do next reveals what you truly believe. If you trust Him completely and follow His lead, then you will experience the spins, twirls, and lifts of the glory life Jesus came to give. If you decide to sit this one out because of fear, then the chairs along the wall are positioned just for you to sit and watch the less fearful wow the crowd. But know this; the band is playing your song.

When God extends His invitation to join Him in the divine dance of obedience, the time to accept is at that very moment. We have about ten to thirty seconds before common sense talks us out of obeying God's promptings. The time to act is as soon as you sense the Spirit calling you to move.

We often act as if we have all the time in the world to respond to God's invitation to obedience. But world history does not stand still on our account. It will not wait for us to make up our minds. The world turns. The days pass. Time moves on. We either accept the invitation or sit out the dance of a lifetime.

John told me about a missed opportunity that he would always regret.

"I heard that a friend of mine was in the hospital because of a spider bite," he began. "As soon as I heard it, I thought, *I should go by the hospital and see him.* But then I decided I would just wait until he came home from the hospital and run by his house. A few days later, I heard he had died. I was heartsick. If I had only obeyed God's nudge at the very moment He prompted me to go, rather than rationalizing the prompting away. The hospital was only a few miles away. I'll never forget that missed opportunity to minister to a friend because I chose to ignore God's prompting."

At some point in your relationship with Jesus, God will invite you to join Him in His work. It may seem like an impossible task. That's when you will have a decision to make. You can either accept the invitation or reject it. This is the critical point where many decide to remain in cold metal seats of complacency and watch others move around the dance floor in breathtaking beauty. Then they wonder why they do not experience God working in and through their lives as other Christians do. They wonder why others talk about moments of sudden glory while their own lives seem lacking.

Perhaps you feel that you are not good enough, smart enough, or talented enough for God to use in mighty ways. God loves inviting the incapable to show that He is capable. He delights in choosing the unqualified to show that He is more than qualified. He loves choosing the weak to show that He is strong. So if you feel inadequate in your own gifts and abilities, congratulations, you are exactly the person God is looking for to show Himself mighty.

Rick Warren, in his book *The Purpose Driven Life,* reminds us of some very unlikely dance partners that God invited to take a spin.

Abraham was old, Jacob was insecure, Leah was unattractive, Joseph was abused, Moses stuttered, Gideon was poor, Samson was codependent, Rahab was immoral, David had an affair and all kinds of family problems, Elijah was suicidal, Jeremiah was depressed, Jonah was reluctant, Naomi was a widow, John the Baptist was eccentric to say the least, Peter was impulsive and hot-tempered, Martha worried a lot, the Samaritan woman had several failed marriages, Zacchaeus was unpopular, Thomas had doubts, Paul had poor health, and Timothy was timid. That's quite a group of misfits, but God used each of them in his service. He will use you too.[33]

I love this scenario. The religious leaders were listening to Peter and John preach. They were perplexed; astonished, really. They wondered where Peter and John acquired such knowledge and wisdom. "When they saw the courage of Peter and John and realized that they were unschooled, ordinary men, they were astonished and they *took note that these men had been with Jesus*" (Acts 4:13).

Ah, *they had been with Jesus.* That explained everything.

We tend to look at folks who are talented or who have great resources and think, "If we could win that soul for the Lord, then think of all he could accomplish for the kingdom." How silly. As if God needs our meager resources to accomplish anything.

When you say yes to God despite your inabilities, then you become a living, breathing, walking display of His glory as you *live and move and have your being in Him.* "But God chose the foolish things of the world to shame the wise; God chose the weak things of the world to shame the strong. He chose the lowly things of this world and the despised things—and the things that are not—to nullify the things that are, so that no one may boast before him" (1 Corinthians 1:27–29).

You are always one step of obedience away from the next great adventure and moments of sudden glory that follow. Are you willing to abandon that which makes you comfortable to embrace that which makes you fulfilled? Are you ready for the fancy footwork of faith?

As you consider joining Jesus on the dance floor of obedience, remember this: "The one who calls you is faithful and he will do it" (1 Thessalonians 5:24). Don't worry that you don't know all the right moves. He does. You simply need to follow His lead. *In Him we live and move and have our being*…the dance of obedience is breathtakingly beautiful.

SMOOTH DANCE MOVES

Perhaps you are thinking, *But Sharon, I thought you said that we tend to make the Christian life too hard or too difficult. Obedience sounds hard to me.*

Obedience may seem that way at first, but in reality, obedience is the easy way. It is difficult to cope with the messes we get into when we don't obey. The consequences of sin are hard to deal with. Think about the times you have disobeyed or turned your back on God. What were the results? Easy? Hard?

Satan will try to convince you that obedience is much too hard, that it carries too high a price, but he will never tell you the cost of not obeying God. He will never tell you the glory moments you will forfeit by refusing or ignoring God's invitation to join Him.

Practicing Acts 17:28 will never lead to sin. When we wrangle from God's embrace and set out on our own, that's when we get in trouble. God isn't telling us to obey to make life difficult. God wants us to obey to make life *less* difficult. The end result of obedience is the blessed way...smooth moves.

Jesus said, "Come to Me, all who are weary and heavy-laden, and I will give you rest. Take My yoke upon you and learn from Me.... For My yoke is easy and My burden is light" (Matthew 11:28–30, NASB). The yoke is simply a farmer's understanding of the divine dance of obedience. When two oxen are yoked together, they move as one— walking in tandem to the bidding of the master. Usually, an older, more experienced animal is yoked with a young upstart. The apprentice ox learns from the more seasoned ox as they walk along tethered together. If the younger animal tries to surge ahead, the yoke chokes at his neck and slows him down. If he lags behind, the yoke chafes at his neck and prods him to hurry along.

And what does Jesus say about this yoke? It is not hard. It is not difficult. It is not heavy. It is easy. It is light. Being yoked to Jesus actually makes life much simpler...smoother...more peace-filled.

God said to the people of Israel: "If only you had paid attention to my commands, your peace would have been like a river, your righteousness like the waves of the sea" (Isaiah 48:18). A river flows unhindered over rocks and boulders as it moves from one place to the next. It flows around them, over them, and past them—all the while smoothing rough edges. A river doesn't strive to get from one place to another. It simply flows. That is the glory life of *living and moving and having our being in Christ*. We simply flow with a sacred inner calmness. Sometimes circumstances will be like tumultuous white-capped rapids, other times like a lazy, gentle stream. But the life in union with Jesus keeps flowing. Moving forward. And in the journey, we catch glimpses of sudden glory in the scenery as we move between life's banks.

Obedience is so much more than following a list of dos and don'ts. Practicing religion rather than enjoying a love relationship with Jesus is like trying to plow the field alone. It will exhaust you rather than energize you. You will feel like a martyr and then wonder why others around you seem to be so joyful in their calling. Obedience because of our love relationship energizes our lives. Obedience out of a sense of duty or law drains. Always drains.

Religion operates on a works-of-the-law principle: "I obey God, therefore, I am accepted by God." Relationship operates on the gospel-of-grace principle: "I am accepted by God through the finished work of Jesus, therefore I obey—because I love and trust Him." We're going to talk more about that in chapter 8. This is important to understand because until we grasp the difference, we will never experience the joy of *living and moving and having our being in Christ.*

Obedience is a *response* to love. Jesus said, "If anyone loves me, he will obey my teaching. My Father will love him, and we will come to him and make our home with him. He who does not love me will not obey my teaching" (John 14:23–24).

Sometimes relinquishing control and following Jesus's lead through obedience can feel uncertain or awkward, like when your dance partner leads you into a new move for the very first time. But each time you say yes to God, a new passion and peace flows through your veins until eventually, hopefully, a total transfusion of Christ-centered living replaces self-centered stubbornness. Intimacy becomes sweeter. Passion grows stronger. Glory moments become easier to see. Unique glory moments…selected especially for you.

UNIQUE CHOREOGRAPHY

Have you ever looked at someone's life and thought, *I want to do what she's doing. I want to have the impact on others that she is having. I want the ministry she has.* Unfortunately, I have fallen into that trap many times. But then God reminds me of His words: "I know the plans I have for *you*" (Jeremiah 29:11). His plan for me is uniquely choreographed. His plan for you is uniquely choreographed...planned to a T.

I recall watching a crowd of line dancers at a wedding reception. The bridesmaids queued on the dance floor as music pulsated through the room. Synchronized movements began as the girls shuffled to the right, shuffled to the left, kicked right, kicked left. Toe-tap-turn. Onlookers jumped in, and soon two lines of wedding-goers, both young and old, herded from left to right as the disc jockey's music prodded them along.

There was no leader in this line dance. Everyone seemed to be on his or her own—dancers mistakenly thinking they were independent but simply doing what everyone else was doing. They had smiles on their faces and swaggers in their gaits. Onlookers admired their moves. I watched the dancers, but I saw the world.

Not that this bunch was particularly worldly, but I saw a portrayal of the world's movements on the tiny dance floor—a crowd of men and women shuffling about, independent from one another, yet mimicking each other's moves. Line dancers on the dance floor of life with no leader, simply a mass of movement to the world's rhythm.

Don't get me wrong; I'm not against line dancing. This was just a startling vision as I considered God's children mimicking one another, or at least trying to. It made me sad. It caused me to ponder my own tendency to fall in line and leave my dance partner standing against the wall. Oh, that we would step out of the world's parade and *live and move and have our being in Jesus.*

God has specific dreams and plans choreographed for each of His children. We were not created for a celestial line dance with everyone moving in the same direction. We can look at how He has worked in someone else's life and try our best to duplicate what she did and how she did it, but we will not get the same results. How He works in one person's life may be completely different from how He works in yours. If we trust in methods rather than in God, we limit the way we will experience Him. He is much more complex, creative, and innovative than we can possibly conceive.

As far as I know, God spoke through a burning bush only once. God spoke through a donkey only once. He wrote on a wall only once. That doesn't mean that He can't or won't use those miraculous means to speak to you and to me, but it does mean that we shouldn't expect Him to give a repeat performance when He has infinite ways to make Himself known.

In Him we live and move and have our being is the hope for all of us, but just where and how that moving about in God takes place will be distinctively designed just for you. Sometimes the choreography will make perfect sense in your limited understanding, and other times it may make no sense at all. But be sure of this: God always has a plan.

Put on Your Dancing Shoes

Sometimes we are hesitant to join God on the dance floor because it just doesn't make sense. It didn't make sense for Noah to build an ark when it had never rained on the earth before. It didn't make sense for stuttering Moses to become the spokesperson for the Jewish nation. It didn't make sense for a bunch of uneducated fishermen to be God's chosen ambassadors to spread the gospel throughout the world. And sister, sometimes what God asks you to do will make no sense at all to your limited understanding and finite mind. And if you choose to follow despite your lack of understanding, many glory moments await just around the bend of obedience.

One particular day, God asked me to do something that made no sense to me. I had gone through the drive-through at Chick-fil-A, and the cashier said, "Oh, I love that shirt you have on today!"

"Thanks," I replied as I received my sweet tea. "Have a great day!"

No sooner had I taken a sip of liquid South when God impressed something on my heart.

Go and buy that girl the same shirt you have on, He seemed to say.

Now God, that's silly, I argued. *She'll think I'm strange.*

Go and buy that girl the same shirt you have on, He repeated.

They probably don't even have this shirt anymore. I got it weeks ago.

Go and buy that girl the same shirt you have on, He said again.

"Daggumit," I muttered as I steered my car toward T.J. Maxx.

Sure enough, there was that same shirt, in my Chick-fil-A friend's size, just hanging there smiling at me. I felt rather silly at the checkout counter purchasing the very blouse that I was wearing. I was hoping the cashier wouldn't ask any questions. She didn't, but she didn't make eye contact either.

I made my purchase, wrapped the blouse up in a gift bag with curling ribbon, and drove back to Chick-fil-A. The gal was still there...of course. I called her over and began to question her.

"Is today your birthday?" I asked.

"No," she replied.

"Have you had a particularly bad day?" I queried.

"No," she answered again.

"Well, I don't know why, but God told me to go out and buy this blouse for you. You might think I'm the strangest person you've ever met, but I had to obey Him. Consider this a gift from Jesus today. Hope you enjoy it."

She took the gift and gave me a hug.

Now, if you are waiting for the miraculous punch line, there isn't one. I wasn't the answer to her prayers, at least not that I know of. She didn't send in my name to the newspaper as her hero for the day. As far as I know, nothing extraordinary ever came of me buying her that shirt. I just did it. She just took it.

Why did I tell you this uneventful, unmoving story? See, when we erase the lines between the secular and the sacred, when we sense God's presence in every moment of every day, He will place opportunities to join Him in the divine dance of obedience throughout our days. Divine appointments stand in front of us in the grocery store line. Divine appointments sit beside us on airplanes. Divine appointments wave at us across a crowded room. They might not be earth-shattering or life-changing feats. But let me assure you of this: when you enter the divine dance of obedience, the heavenly hosts applaud and your dance partner smiles.

And here is a thought to ponder: even though your act of obedience may not result in a glory moment for you, it may be a glory moment in someone else's life. I don't know about you, but that takes my breath away.

Accepting God's invitation to the divine dance of obedience often means taking a leap of faith, and it's worth saying again: we will always have a choice.

TAKING A LEAP OF FAITH

Several years ago, on a trip to Kauai, my husband and our friends Larry and Cynthia Price decided to go on a zip line through the jungle. After being jostled and tossed like ragdolls in the back of a retired army jeep, we finally made it to the top of the mountain from which we were going to zip down—risking life and limb, I might add.

I hopped out of the jeep and eyed the cable suspended high above the valley below. After watching Cynthia fly through the trees, I climbed up onto a wooden platform and surrendered to Jack, a jovial, burly Hawaiian, who strapped me into a harness and placed a helmet on my head. With a simple click of a metal buckle, he attached my harnessed body onto a seemingly flimsy steel cable. As I stood on the edge of the platform eyeing the disappearing earth below my feet, I had a choice. I could say, "no thanks," and ask to be released from the cable, or I could jump.

I chose to jump. My body flew over the treetops and the stunningly beautiful gorge. I was Tarzan's Jane, and this was my jungle. Airborne. Exhilarating. Risky.

Jacob was with us that day. He was a stranger among our little band of adventurers. Jacob was alone. No friends. No spouse. No family.

"Jacob, what brings you up to this mountain today?" I asked.

"I'm afraid of heights," he answered.

I then noticed the thin line of perspiration beading over his upper lip. The slight tremble in his voice. The mechanical one-foot-in-front-of-the-other halted gait up the hill.

"You're afraid of heights?" I asked. "Then why are you here?"

"I'm going to conquer it today," he answered determinedly.

I was struck. We were here to have fun. He was here for a totally different reason. When Jacob stood on that platform, I prayed for my new friend. For Jacob this was not just a joyride…or just maybe it was.

I'm not saying that God told Jacob to go to the top of a mountain, attach his body to a flimsy cable, and fly over the gorge at the risk of life and limb. But I am saying that obedience often requires a leap of faith. Too often we say yes to God but live the no because of fear. We stand at the precipice of belief, and a decision has to be made. Am I going to trust God or not? Am I going to attach my heart to the cable of His love and take a leap of faith, or am I going to freeze in fear because I don't trust that He has my best interest in mind? Am I going to settle for safety and miss the thrill of seeing God work through me?

As we *live and move and have our being* in Jesus, God will take us to some amazing places. And there will always be a choice. Will we jump headlong into the adventurous journey of His perfect plan, or will we hang back for lack of faith? Jacob stood on the platform, took a deep breath, and jumped. He flew over the treetops, careened over the river, and landed safely on the other side of his greatest fear.

We clapped and cheered. Jacob took a bow. God smiled.

In Him we live and move and have our being…and sometimes we soar.

7

Trusting God in Tough Times

As the heavens are higher than the earth, so
are my ways higher than your ways and my
thoughts than your thoughts.
—Isaiah 55:9

I sat on the floor playing a card game with my young son. It was
shaping up to be one of the best summers ever. Steven was savoring
every minute of the long hot days, our golden retriever, Ginger, had
delivered seven adorable puppies, and after years of negative pregnancy
tests and doctor visits, I had a new life growing in my womb.

In the middle of enjoying the moment with Steven, I felt a warm,
sticky sensation that made my world stand still. A trip to the bathroom
confirmed my greatest fear.

Later that day, as I sat in the doctor's office listening to his condo-
lences for the loss of this much-prayed-for child, all I could think was,
God, how could you?

I drove home. Climbed into bed. Pulled the covers over my empty womb and my empty heart and cried. I was mad at God. *If this is how You love me, then forget it.* I gave God the silent treatment, as if I could somehow pay Him back.

God and I had a lover's quarrel that summer. Actually, I was the only one arguing. I was mad. I was hurt. I felt betrayed by the one who was supposed to love me most. But He stayed right by my side, waiting, wooing, and eventually drawing my broken heart back so that He could heal it once again. His passionate pursuit and relentless romance continued.

Even though I was mad at God, I knew in the deepest parts of myself that He did love me and that He was somehow going to use all this pain for good—but I sure didn't like it.

Ann Voskamp wrote: "I wonder…if the rent in the canvas of our life's backdrop, the losses that puncture our world, our own emptiness, might actually become places to see. To see through to God."[34] This was a see-through place, but until I opened my eyes, I would not see God.

Could it be that the puncture wounds in the canvas of your life—the losses, the disappointments, the crushing blows—might actually become the rent places of the soul through which you can see God? Through which you can peer beyond your earthly trappings into glory moments beyond? Through which you can see His light bursting through the openings? I believe they *could* be.

How do we allow life's difficulties to become see-through places? How do we begin to see moments of sudden glory burst through the puncture holes in the black backdrop of our greatest disappointments and pain?

Seeing Beyond the Veil

As you *live and move and have your being* in Christ, at some point, difficult days will come. We live in a fallen world, and suffering is simply a part of it. Jesus said, "In this world you will have trouble" (John 16:33). It's a sure thing.

When we experience shattered dreams, broken relationships, tragic losses, or unfulfilled longings, it can be difficult to feel God's presence, to see His hand, and to hear His voice. Glory moments cease when we close our eyes in pain and tune God out in anger. That doesn't mean that God is not there. It only means that the sadness in our own hearts has drawn the shades and locked the doors. We question whether or not we even want to live in union with God if this is where the path leads. We tend to wriggle out of His arms like an angry child or slip out of His embrace like a disgruntled lover, all the while hoping He will pull us back in and tell us that we have simply misunderstood.

Men and women throughout the Bible voiced their disappointment when God didn't act as they had hoped. David cried out, "My God, my God, why have you forsaken me? Why are you so far from saving me, so far from the words of my groaning?" (Psalm 22:1). Habakkuk cried out, "How long, O LORD, must I call for help, but you do not listen?" (1:2). Even Jesus, when He hung on that cruel Roman cross, did not call out the comforting words of the Twenty-third Psalm but the agonizing words of the Twenty-second.

Philip Yancey, in his book *Disappointment with God,* writes, "The words of the prophets sound like the words of a lovers' quarrel drifting through thin apartment walls."[35] I've read the words. I've heard the words. I've said the words.

And while we complain of God's silence or seeming indifference during difficult times, He is always there working behind the scenes in ways we may never understand.

In the Bible, we catch glimpses of God's veiled activity among men. Daniel prayed for three weeks while God appeared to be silent. Finally an angel showed up and explained his delay—a demon, the prince of the Persian kingdom, had fought with him and held him back for twenty-one days (see Daniel 10:2–13).

In another incident, the prophet Elisha and his servant were surrounded by Aramean enemies. Elisha's servant was terrified and thought they were surely doomed. Elisha very calmly reassured him: "Don't be afraid…. Those who are with us are more than those who are with them." Then he asked God to lift the curtain of the spiritual realm and reveal the truth of the situation. "Then the LORD opened the servant's eyes, and he looked and saw the hills full of horses and chariots of fire all around Elisha" (2 Kings 6:15–17). Talk about sudden glory!

Three months after the loss of my second child, I broke my silence with God and prayed a prayer similar to Elisha's. "Oh, God, please open my eyes to see Your glory in this situation. If I could just see her. Please, Lord, give me a glimpse."

And then God pulled back the curtain in my mind, and I envisioned this child, healthy and whole and playing at the feet of Jesus. She was surrounded by God's glory face to face. Radiant, resplendent glory. Not an ounce of glory ache to be seen.

Glory moments do not require a physical vision but a spiritual revelation—an understanding of a greater reality than this physical world in which we live.

The unseen world is very real, and while we may not see God's activity with our physical eyes, we can be assured of His provision and protection in ways we may never understand. When He said, "I will never leave you or forsake you," He meant it (see Hebrews 13:5).

"So we fix our eyes not on what is seen [our circumstances], but on what is unseen [God's presence]. For what is seen is temporary, but what is unseen is eternal" (2 Corinthians 4:18). One day, it will all make sense. Until then…we trust. And when we have the faith to keep our eyes open during the dark times, God will scatter moments of sudden glory like stars in the inky sky. We hold fast and continue practicing Acts 17:28—even when we aren't sure where that may lead.

Knowing God Sees You

Let's face it. People let us down. They disappoint us. And so does God. Often our experiences fall short of our expectations for God to meet all our needs the way we think He should, and like a lover who has been wronged, we tend to guard our hearts against future disappointment by lowering our expectations and trust. But make no mistake about it, God sees. God understands. He is not aloof.

One day I was sitting on the patio with my friend Beth and her stepfather, Sam, waiting for the grill to heat up before placing steaks on to cook. Beth's mom opened the door and gave Sam his orders—telling him what to do and how to do it. When she went back inside, Sam made a hand signal, pointing in one ear and out the other. We all three laughed. Then he placed his ruddy hand on Beth's arm, a hand worn by years of working under the hood of cars of every make and model.

"She was pretty hard on you growing up, wasn't she?" he asked.

"You have no idea," Beth answered with a sigh.

But Sam did have an idea. He understood. And that one simple gesture let her know that he had peered into her heart and had seen the truth. The weathered, uneducated country mechanic had looked under the hood of her heart with wisdom and seen the damaged engine within. A heart, though healed by Christ, that still felt the phantom pains of a little girl who felt she was never good enough, who was constantly told what to do and how to do it—and who never did it quite right. Sam saw her heart, and for that, Beth loved him. And so did I.

How like God. He places His hand on your shoulders, looks into your eyes, and lets you know that He understands. "I see you," He says. "I see what you are going through." Like Hagar who experienced a sudden glory moment with God in the desert, we too can know God as *El Roi,* "the God who sees me" (Genesis 16:13).

The book of Hebrews tells us that we have a high priest, Jesus, who understands what we are going through. He "sympathizes" with our weakness (Hebrews 4:15). The word *sympathize* comes from two Greek words, *sym* and *pathos,* meaning "suffer with." We are not alone in our suffering, and there are glory moments to be found in the dark if we will keep our eyes open to see.

God did not write the story of your life and then sit back to watch it play out. He is in the story with you. As a matter of fact, He has the leading role. Oh, we try to butt in and take the spotlight. We try to push Him out of the way and take over the lead. But when we get to heaven and look at the playbill, we will see that God had the leading role all along and our names were there in supporting roles as a display of His glory. Oh, if we only knew.

Trusting in His Ultimate Plan

Steve and I got married when we were both still in college. He was entering his fourth year of dental school, and I was just a few hours shy of completing my degree. The last year of school held many important decisions for us, such as where Steve would set up his practice. Dentists don't tend to move about, so this was an important, probably lifelong decision for both of us.

All year we prayed, researched, and weighed various opportunities and options. Finally, in April of that year, we felt God calling us to Pineville, North Carolina, right outside of Charlotte. A dentist there was looking for a young associate, and the pieces of the puzzle began falling into place. We had prayed. We had fasted. We had listened. We felt that this was God's answer for our lives. It was a big deal.

So after graduation, we packed our meager belongings and moved to Charlotte. After setting up house in our tiny apartment, Steve went to meet with the doctor to finalize the work schedule and management particulars.

"Steve, I've been thinking about it," the doctor began, "and I don't think this is such a good idea after all. I've changed my mind."

He extended his hand to my twenty-five-year-old stunned husband and said, "Good luck to you, son."

I was surprised when Steve came home much earlier than I expected. "What are you doing home?" I asked.

"Sit down," he managed. "You're not going to believe this."

Steve told me the story, and I was shocked. I was disappointed. A host of raw emotions collided with questions for God. *How could You do this? How could we have been so wrong? Didn't we hear You correctly?*

We prayed. We fasted. We wanted nothing more than to do what You wanted us to do, where You wanted us to do it. Now here we sit in a big city, with a big student loan and no job. Now what are we supposed to do?

This was a lover's quarrel, my friend, and guess whose voice was the loudest? I felt as though I had kept my part of the bargain by following all the right steps and saying all the right words, but God had not kept His.

Somehow, we've come up with the absurd idea that God owes us. That He is obliged to reveal Himself in a way that is acceptable…that fosters belief. If we do A and B, then He is obliged to do C. He's not. One glance at Job chapters 38–41 puts my silly demands in proper perspective. "Where were you when I laid the earth's foundation?" God questioned Job. "Who marked off its dimensions?… Who shut up the sea behind doors when it burst forth from the womb, when I made the clouds its garment and wrapped it in thick darkness.… Have you ever given orders to the morning, or shown the dawn its place…?" (38:4–5, 8–9, 12). (If you haven't read those chapters lately, they are a great reminder of God's magnificent glory.)

This career setback seems rather petty now as I hear of the tragic losses from hundreds of women who write to me every day. But I have discovered that the accumulations of petty disappointments tend to undermine our faith like little termites gnawing away at the foundation of our lives. They can leave us doubting whether or not God is really concerned about the everyday details of our lives. A lava flow of doubt covers over our faith and we wonder, *Why should I pray at all?*

Our limited vision doesn't allow us to see *how* God is working behind the scenes in our lives. But we must believe that He is.

Each and every trial is an opportunity to trust Him more. Jean Pierre de Caussade said it well:

> You would be very ashamed if you knew what experiences you call setbacks, upheavals, pointless disturbances, and tedious annoyances really are. You would realize that your complaints about them are nothing more nor less than blasphemies—though that never occurs to you. Nothing happens to you except by the will of God, and yet [God's] beloved children curse it because they do not know it for what it is.[36]

His ways are higher than our ways and His thoughts higher than our thoughts (Isaiah 55:9).

If it were up to me, I would have written some stories differently. I would have a little girl who would be twenty-one years old this year. Carol's son would not be in prison. Linda's twenty-year-old daughter would not be a quadriplegic because of a car crash at a tollbooth when she was a toddler. Barbara's daughter would not be bipolar. Patty's twenty-one-year-old daughter would not have died in a car accident. Jennifer's husband would not have died of a brain tumor. If I had been writing the story…

But I'm so glad I'm not the author of those stories. Each and every one of these friends have ministries that impact thousands upon thousands of women all over the world. God has turned their pain into purpose, their misery into ministry, and their devastation into anointed messages of hope and restoration. Sudden glories fill and spill from each of these women's lives. Their love journeys of *living and moving and having their being in Christ* have led them through dark valleys and back out into the light on the other side. They practically glow with radiant wonder.

Difficult times are pregnant with glory moments just waiting to be birthed in the lives of those willing to labor through the pain. The key is to not allow bitterness and anger to make our hearts infertile to God's gifts. One way to avoid the darkening of the soul is by constant communication seasoned with thanksgiving—a continual acknowledgment of His presence.

Glory moments in difficult times are not dependent on our circumstances but on our focus. Focus on the difficulty, and God is difficult to see. Focus on God, and glory seeps through the broken places. Difficulties become the bass notes of our life's song, adding a depth and beauty not found in a life that hovers about middle C.

Steve and I were terribly disappointed, and we felt stranded in a new city with no job and no income. However, after the doctor changed his mind about Steve joining his practice, we never went hungry. I worked six days a week in various dental offices, and Steve filled in where he could. Then, three months later, a situation opened up in a very desirable part of town with one of the city's most respected doctors. Steve was offered a wonderful situation in which to begin his career. If we had written out the best-case scenario ourselves, it would not have come close to what God provided. It was Ephesians 3:20 in lab-coat white: "Now to him who is able to do immeasurably more than all we ask or imagine, according to his power that is at work within us..."

After a few years, the part of town in which we originally planned to set up Steve's practice became a rundown thoroughfare, and that doctor faded away. However, Steve's practice continued to grow and grow and grow, until we had to move out on our own to expand. We experienced God's provision and protection through the twists and turns of uncertainty.

Well, why didn't God do that in the first place? Why didn't He lead us to that second opportunity when we did all that praying and seeking? He could have. But He is far more interested in developing our character than doling out a life of comfort and ease. C. S. Lewis notes: "If you think of this world as a place intended simply for our happiness, you find it quite intolerable: think of it as a place of training and correction and it's not so bad."[37] We are ever the students. God is the teacher still. Trials rip away the flimsy fabric of self-sufficiency and become the raw material for God's miracles in our lives. And those miracles are a sudden glory.

A year later, I sat thanking God for His provision, and I was ashamed of myself. Ashamed that I had doubted God. Ashamed that I had fussed at Him. Ashamed that I had thrown a temper tantrum when I didn't get what I wanted when I wanted it…and I'm so glad I didn't.

"I'm so sorry, God," I prayed. "Please forgive me."

That's okay, He seemed to say. *Happens all the time. Now, I want this to be a lesson for you. You've got to trust Me.*

Author Phillip Yancey wrote, "Faith means believing in advance what will only make sense in reverse." Oh, that we would trust Him even if the twists and turns never make sense this side of heaven. That's what trusting God is all about. As *we live and move and have our being in Him,* the dark places are simply opportunities to trust that He knows the way—and the perfect time to hold on tight.

FINDING PURPOSE IN THE PAIN

Of all the roles Grainne (pronounced like Sonya) had in life, being a mother was her greatest love. A houseful of boys—Pierce, twin boys Garrett and Killian, and Finnian—was always an adventure.

When Killian was five years old, he got a stomachache that would not go away. The doctors ran a blood test and discovered something that would rock the family's world forever. Killian had leukemia. By all appearances, he was a healthy, happy boy with big green eyes and a full head of curly blond hair. "How could he have cancer?" Grainne cried. "This only happens in the movies and on television, not to our little boy!"

Grainne and Killian and their family embarked on a long journey of chemotherapy and its horrible side effects—mouth sores, hair loss, nausea, pain, weakness, and isolation in hospital rooms. But Killian never wanted to be treated like he was sick. He insisted on playing sports throughout his years of treatment: baseball, basketball, and swimming. One day he participated in a swim meet only a few hours after having a spinal tap and got upset when he came in third.

Watching Killian suffer, Grainne wondered if this was how God felt watching Jesus die on the cross. All she could do was love him and watch.

Killian ushered in many moments of sudden glory during his battle with leukemia. "One day the nurses had to give Killian two doses of meds—with one syringe in each thigh," Grainne relayed. "I was holding his hands because he was so scared of needles. He screamed and tears poured down his cheeks. The nurses were crying. I was crying.

When he saw our tears, he suddenly stopped crying and repeated, 'Thank you! Thank you! Thank you!' He was more concerned with our crying than his fear. Such love and compassion coming from one so small took my breath away."

After three years of chemotherapy, Killian relapsed. His survival rate dropped from 75 percent to about 30 percent. His best chance for recovery was a bone marrow transplant. The entire family was tested, and his twin brother, Garrett, was a perfect match. After more chemo and radiation, with all the horrific side effects that followed, Killian received the bone marrow transplant and was placed in isolation for nine weeks. The procedure was a success.

"But sometimes leukemia is tougher than even a nine-year-old boy," Grainne explained. "Ninety days posttransplant—just ten days short of the point that a transplant is considered successful—a routine blood test showed the leukemia had returned. The following week, Killian's doctor told us we were out of options and that Killian had about two months to live. He said we should go make some memories while Killian was still well enough to enjoy himself. So we went to Disney World. That was one of the hardest weeks of my life. My heart broke every time I looked at Killian."

Grainne was still not ready to give up. When she returned from her trip to Disney World, she read about a new drug being developed for chemo-resistant childhood leukemia. The drug, BL22, was designed to attach itself only to the cancer cells and destroy them without destroying healthy cells. She called the doctors and asked if Killian could try the drug.

"I'm sorry, Grainne," they said. "This drug is not open to clinical trials for children."

That didn't stop Grainne. She contacted a doctor at the National Cancer Institute and got special permission from the FDA to use the new drug just for Killian. Within a week they were in Maryland, where Killian became the first child in the world to try this new drug. It worked well enough to stop the leukemia cells from multiplying for a short time, but because the drug was experimental, the doctors were not allowed to give Killian a big enough dose to cure him. A second generation of the drug was still being tested in the lab, but they did not have the money to fund the development and get it into treatment. So there it sat…because of a lack of funds.

Over the next few weeks, Killian deteriorated rapidly. His strong spirit kept him alive to see his little brother's sixth birthday. After Finn's celebration, Killian told his parents, "I'm ready to go now."

"Where are you going?" Grainne asked.

"I'm going home."

On Sunday, July 27, 2003, Killian went home.

After Killian's death, Grainne was depressed and angry at God. She felt as though she lived in a deep, dark hole and didn't even want to come out. On the first anniversary of Killian's "homegoing," she tried to comfort his brothers. "Sons, Killian is free of pain and with his heavenly Father, who loves him even more than we ever could."

Suddenly, as these words came out of Grainne's mouth, she had a moment of sudden glory. God spoke to her heart. *Do you believe that, Grainne? He is here with Me, and I do love him more than you ever could. Do you really believe it?*

Grainne knew that if she did truly believe those words, she needed to climb out of her black hole of anger and depression and ask God what He wanted her to do. When she did, He told her.

"I remembered that drug stuck in the lab because of a lack of funding, and I knew I had to make it available to other children," she explained. "We created a program called Coaches Curing Kids' Cancer. We asked children's sports teams to take the money they collected for their coaches' end-of-season gifts and donate it to the program. In return, we let them choose a CCKC T-shirt, baseball cap, or whistle to present to their coach along with a personalized certificate. The proceeds went to pediatric cancer research."

So far, at the writing of this book, they have donated well over $2 million to cancer research for kids. They have been able to fund innovative therapies in hospitals all over the country. And it all began with a little boy named Killian and his family *as they lived and moved and had their being* in God, who always has a purpose and a plan. A God who turns our darkest nights into His most majestic displays of glorious splendor. A God who allows us to participate and become displays of His glory for the world to see.

During the Christmas season of 2010, Killian's doctor handed Grainne a piece of paper. "Here's your Christmas present," he said with a smile. It was the results of the first phase of treatment with the second generation of the drug Killian had pioneered and which Coaches Curing Kids' Cancer had helped fund. The paper listed three children who had gone into complete remission as a direct result of receiving the drug.

"Killian's doctor was wrong," she smiled. "It wasn't just a Christmas present. It was the most wonderful blessing I ever could have imagined."

"During the eight years since Killian lost his battle with leukemia," Grainne said, "my faith has allowed me to see that good things can come from bad. There are glory moments in every dark night.

Through the gift of Killian, my family and I were shown what a difference one short life can make, especially when it is lived with joy and hope. I am just a wife and a mother—no one special. But I have tasted God's grace, seen His power, and heard His still small voice that pushes me to use what I have gone through to help others."*

A sudden glory!

BELIEVING GOD KNOWS BEST

When bad things happen, such as sweet Killian's cancer, we may never understand why. God tells us, "'For my thoughts are not your thoughts, neither are your ways my ways,' declares the LORD. 'As the heavens are higher than the earth, so are my ways higher than your ways and my thoughts than your thoughts'" (Isaiah 55:8–9).

"Trying to analyze His [God's] omnipotence is like an amoeba attempting to comprehend the behavior of man."[38] It's simply not possible. But there is one thing we can be sure of. "All the ways of the LORD are loving and faithful" (Psalm 25:10), whether we understand them or not.

When we encounter difficulties, it is easy to jump to conclusions. We may think God is mad at us or that He is punishing us. We wonder if God is not blessing us because we've disappointed Him in some way. But all through the Bible we see that some of God's closest friends experienced the darkest nights.

Joseph suffered. David suffered. The disciples suffered. Elizabeth suffered. Mary suffered. Martha suffered. Mary (Jesus's mother) suffered.

---

* To learn more about this program, visit www.curingkidscancer.org.

Paul suffered. Jesus suffered. And each one of these men and women were smack-dab in the middle of God's will. The ordinary pabulum of popular religion, of health and prosperity, just doesn't line up with the suffering we see among some of the most godly men and women in Scripture. The abundant life that Jesus came to give does not come without struggle any more than a butterfly can soar without a struggle from its cocoon. We would never slice open a cocoon and expect to find a butterfly ready to fly. Without the struggle, the butterfly could not grow strong enough to take flight.

Jesus warned us that we would have struggles in this life, and yet struggles always seem to catch me by surprise. "Consider it all joy…," James said, "*when* you encounter various trials" (James 1:2, NASB). Notice James said *when* and not *if.* Honestly, I wish there were some other way.

Come to think of it, Jesus wished the same. "My Father, if it is possible, may this cup be taken from me. Yet not as I will, but as you will" (Matthew 26:39). The cross. There was no other way.

Take a look at the names given to the Holy Spirit: Intercessor, Helper, Counselor, and Comforter. The very nature of those names lets us know that we are going to have difficulties this side of heaven, and thankfully God did not leave us to struggle alone. Jesus wept. The Holy Spirit groans. And God's heart aches. In one beautiful sentence, we catch a glimpse into the heart of God as we go through tough times: "In all their distress he too was distressed" (Isaiah 63:9). We may not see God's face during the difficult days of pain, but you can be sure He is there, and many times His face is streaked with tears.

Sometimes life is tough. *In Him we live and move and have our being* does not mean that we will walk down a path void of treacherous twists and turns. It does mean that no matter where the road may lead, we are not alone.

So many times I've cried out with King David, "My God, my God, why have you forsaken me!" only to discover that He was right there with me all the time. None of us knows what the future holds. Sometimes we just need to put our hand in God's and walk around the next corner with Him—even when we don't understand. In that journey into the unknown, we're apt to experience moments of sudden glory in well-placed nuggets of gold.

Several years after the loss of our second child, I stood in the doorframe of my son's bedroom watching him sleep. This sixteen-year-old man-child was six feet long and a tangle of sheets and limbs. One hairy leg hung off the bed, his thick shock of hair was sticking out in every direction, and his face needed a shave. I was struck once again with just how much I loved this boy...my only son.

God, I prayed, *You know how much I love children. Why was there only one? Do You have a nugget of gold for me today?*

Then John 3:16 washed over me like rain: *"For God so loved the world that he gave his one and only Son, that whoever believes in him shall not perish but have eternal life."*

"Is that it, Lord? Is that my nugget of gold?"

Again the words rained down. *"For God so loved the world that he gave his one and only Son, that whoever believes in him shall not perish but have eternal life."*

Tears filled my eyes as I understood God's great sacrifice as never before. Why had I missed it these sixteen years? I have a one and only son. There are many people I love in this world, but there is no one, absolutely no one, that I love enough to give my only son for. And yet, God loved me enough to give *His* Son for me. Not only that, He has given me a living, walking, talking example of that great love every time I see my son's face. If that is the only reason for the years of infertility and loss, then it is enough.

A sudden glory! God's great love took my breath away once again.

Seeing God Through the Lens of Gratitude and Grace

— wonderful hymn

> Come, Thou Fount of ev'ry blessing. Tune
> my heart to sing Thy grace.
> —Robert Robinson, 1757

Enter his gates with thanksgiving and his courts with praise"
(Psalm 100:4). Right in the center of my Bible, I find an invitation into God's presence. And while we have already established that there is nowhere we can go away from God's presence, we can certainly *feel* distant from Him.

In chapter 1, we looked at Adam and Eve's original sin of disobedience to God's one command not to eat from the Tree of the Knowledge of Good and Evil. But have you ever wondered what whet their appetite for wanting something more than constant communion and union with God? Have you ever considered what stirred the desire for more and made them vulnerable to the serpent's enticing suggestion? I think it was ingratitude. They were not thankful for all that God had provided. They were not satisfied with the glory life. So when Satan slithered into the garden and introduced the idea that God was holding out on them, they were ripe for the picking.

"When you eat of it your eyes will be opened," the serpent hissed (Genesis 3:5). But in the beginning, Eve's eyes already were open. Eve saw God in all His goodness, spilling out gifts at every turn. She saw nothing *but* the glory of God unspoiled. Eve was lured away by the lie that there was something better, something more. "When you eat of it your eyes will be opened"…and they were. Eve's eyes beheld the ugliness of sin and shame that she had never seen before.

We are in the same danger of believing Satan's lie of "you would be happy if…" when we are not grateful to God, who "richly blesses all who call on him" (Romans 10:12). We are vulnerable to temptation when we neglect to thank God, who "richly provides us with everything for our enjoyment" (1 Timothy 6:17).

As *we live and move and have our being* in Jesus, if the song of gratitude is not playing on our lips, we will be in the same danger of listening to the Enemy's lies and thinking our glory ache could be satisfied by something other than God Himself. Gratitude keeps us grounded in the truth and alert to the lies.

Ingratitude is the infection of Eden that shuts our eyes tight to glory moments and leaves us groping about in the dark for that which will never satisfy the longings of the soul. The cure comes in capsules of praise, thanksgiving, and a grateful heart. Gratitude is the antibiotic of the soul to cure a variety of the world's ills. It cuts the bark of our hard hearts, nourishes the very spot where we are grafted into Jesus Christ Himself, and restores a sense of closeness and intimacy with God.

THE PRACTICE OF GRATITUDE

Gratitude is the most effective way to deepen your consciousness to the fact that you are the object of God's affection and love. Giving thanks awakens your senses to see God, to hear God, to taste and see that He is good. When you *feel* far from God, praise will bring you back. When you have strayed from acknowledging God's presence, when you have forgotten that *in Him we live and move and have our being,* praise and gratitude will be the ramp to get you back on the right road.

I shudder at the words of Romans chapter 1. "They neither *glorified him as God nor gave thanks to him,* but their thinking became futile and their foolish hearts were darkened" (verse 21). They did not glorify Him. They did not give thanks to Him. "Therefore God gave them over in the sinful desires of their hearts" (verse 24). The light of their eyes went dark.

Praise keeps you alert to the glimpses of glory all around. The more you glorify God with praise and thanksgiving, the more your eyes will be opened to the deep well of His love that is but a bowshot away (see Genesis 21:19). God inhabits the praises of His people (see Psalm 22:3, KJV). He feels right at home in a heart that praises Him. He enjoys being there!

I believe gratitude grows with practice. When you thank God, regardless of your feelings, it primes the pump of your heart until gratitude begins to flow freely.

If this is a language you have not spoken often, you can become fluent…with practice. Paul wrote, "I have *learned* how to be content with whatever I have. I know how to live on almost nothing or with everything" (Philippians 4:11–12, NLT). "I have learned."

As with any foreign language we attempt to learn, the more we use it, the more fluent we become. Is it too strong to say that the language of gratitude is a "foreign" tongue? I don't think so. We come into the world screaming with our very first breath, "It's all about me and my needs!" With tightly closed fists and squeezed-shut eyes we demand attention. A newborn babe can think of nothing more than his wants and his needs: feed me, hold me, change me, nurse me…and do it right now! I would like to think we eventually grow out of that infantile attitude, but I'm sorry to say, many never do.

But we don't have to live like self-centered, self-absorbed ingrates. We can learn God's love language of gratitude that opens our eyes and unfurls our fingers. We can speak words of gratitude that remove our blinders so we can see glimpses of His glory every day. As we discover and practice the beautiful language of gratitude, our native tongue of self-focused dissatisfaction begins to fade.

And we practice. And we practice. And we practice.

I often ask my Spanish-speaking friends who are also fluent in English, "When you dream, do you dream in Spanish or in English?"

Most of the time they say Spanish. A few say both. But only the ones totally immersed in English, who have lived in the States for a long period of time, actually dream in their learned language rather than their native tongue.

Oh, how I long for the tongue of gratitude to become the language of my dreams. My heart language. But that will not happen by putting my Bible under my pillow. It is a result of practice as I *live and move and have my being in Him* with a grateful heart.

THE CONTAGIOUSNESS OF INGRATITUDE

Ingratitude laced with grumbling, complaining, and murmuring is an easy trap to fall into. And it is so contagious. Someone grumbles and the next thing you know, you fall right in line and start grumbling too. I wonder if that's what happened in the wilderness as the Israelites made one more trek around Mount Sinai. "I'm sick of this manna," one complained. Then another looked at God's sweet provision and said, "Come to think of it, I'm sick of it too." The next thing you know the sea of ingrates becomes a tidal wave of grumblers, and God sends them on another lap around the wilderness and places a Do Not Enter sign in front of the Promised Land.

When you think about it, ingratitude is a casual despising of God's sovereignty. It's like saying we don't like how He is running things and think we could do it better.

Gratitude and giving thanks in all things opens our eyes to see God's glory in even the smallest things. On the other hand, ingratitude blinds our eyes to God's presence, and we miss His advances all around. It's a choice, not an emotion. However, this choice to give thanks may very well open the way for positive emotions such as joy to emerge and take hold. Paul wrote: "Rejoice in the Lord always. I will say it again [because you probably didn't get it the first time]: Rejoice!" (Philippians 4:4).

There is nobody more miserable than an ungrateful person. Margaret and I were chatting about gratitude when she mentioned how she tries to steer clear of those who grumble and complain because their ingratitude is so contagious. "I hate calling my sister," she mused. "I mean, I love her. But talking to her is such a joy drain."

"What do you mean?" I asked.

"All she does is complain. Something is always wrong with her house. She always has a new ailment. She gives me the latest obituary report and tells me who is sick with what. A couple of times I tried to cheer her up. You know, help her see the positive side of things. 'At least you have a house. Think of all those people who lost their homes in the hurricane.' But it only made her mad. She said I was not being sympathetic and that I made little of her problems. So now I just listen."

Another friend told me of sitting with his father discussing the distribution of his "worldly goods," when the time came to do so. "My dad had very little joy in his life," Mike explained. "As we discussed who was going to get what when he died, I saw a pride in him I had never noticed before. 'I did all this,' he said as he waved his hand around the room like Vanna White. 'I worked hard and earned it all.' In his mind, *he had earned it; he had done it all.* Never once did he give thanks to God for all his blessings or acknowledge God's goodness. He showed no gratitude, no thanksgiving, and certainly no joy."

His things had become shiny shackles that kept joy at bay all his life. His things. How sad.

As Mike told me the story, I thought of Henry Ward Beecher's words: "Pride slays thanksgiving.... A proud man is seldom a grateful man, for he never thinks he gets as much as he deserves."[39] Eyes shut tight to God's glory.

I am reminded of an old saying that stirs and stings: "Gratitude turns what we have into enough." Always enough. Jesus thanked God for the two loaves and five fish…and there was more than enough to go around (see John 6:1–13).

Gratitude can change your perspective on the simplest of mundane tasks and transform them into moments of sudden glory. One day I was mopping the kitchen floor, and my mood was anything but grateful. I grumbled with each push of the mop. Complained with each dip in the bucket. *Here I am mopping this floor again and no one even appreciates it. I feel like this housework is never finished. Clean today. Dirty tomorrow. Why do I even bother?*

Then right in the middle of the kitchen, God showed up. Actually, He was there all along, but my grumbling blinded the eyes of my heart to recognize His presence. New thoughts began to emerge as I pushed the mop across the linoleum floor. I believe God put them there.

Suppose you were blind and you couldn't see the beautiful patterns on the linoleum floor or the spilled juice by the refrigerator door. Suppose you were deaf and you couldn't hear the soothing sound of the soap bubbles dissolving in the bucket or the rhythmic sound of the mop being pushed back and forth across the floor's hard surface. Suppose you were in a wheelchair and you weren't strong enough to stand upright and grasp the wooden handle in your nimble hands to erase the muddy footprints and make the floor shiny and clean again. Suppose you didn't have a home or a family to clean up after.

Suddenly, my grumbling turned into a song of praise and gratitude. "Thank You, Lord, for the privilege of mopping this dirty floor. Thank You for the health and strength to hold this mop in my strong hands and to wrap my agile fingers around its handle. Thank You for the sight to see the crumbs, the dirt, and the spilled juice. Thank You for the sense of smell to enjoy the clean, fresh scent of the soap in my bucket. Thank You for the many precious feet that will walk through this room and dirty it all up again. And, Lord, thank You for the privilege of having a floor to mop and a family to clean up after."

A sudden glory.

The Perspective of Gratitude

Paul wrote the Thessalonians: "Give thanks in all circumstances" (1 Thessalonians 5:18). We read that verse and think it rather nice. So we slap a sloppy coat of thanksgiving on life and go about our day. In reality, most of us are thankful for very little.

Notice the Bible doesn't command us to *feel* thankful in all circumstances. Instead it commands us to "give thanks in all circumstances." When I begin to praise God in a difficult situation, even if I don't feel like it, many times the scales fall from my eyes and I begin to see glimpses of His glory sprinkled on the black backdrop of the situation like diamonds on black velvet. Sometimes I don't see glory in tragedy, but I still can praise God because I know He is there.

Gratitude changes the lens through which we see the circumstances in our little slice of time. Thanksgiving changes our perspective despite broken dreams, broken relationships, tumultuous circumstances, and unfulfilled longings. As you praise God for who He is and thank Him for what He's done, your perspective of Him grows larger and your problems grow smaller. As a result, you will experience a deeper sense of intimacy with God as the emotional gap between what you know to be true and how you feel at the moment closes.

On many occasions in the Psalms, David complained about his

circumstances (Psalms 42, 57, 62). But more often than not, about midway through David's laments, he begins praising God for who He is and thanking God for what He's done. And you know what happens? All of a sudden David starts feeling better! Life isn't so bad after all! His problems grow smaller as his perspective of God grows larger, and he begins to see God's glory shining through the darkness punctured by praise.

Why is that? In the writing of one little psalm, David shifted from depression to rejoicing. He didn't wait until God changed his situation, solved his problem, or made him feel better before he began thanking Him. Oh, friend, when we stop complaining and grumbling and begin speaking God's love language of gratitude, our perspective will change as well. We will begin seeing moments of sudden glory through the lens of praise and thanksgiving—glory moments that were there all along but hidden from the grumbling eye.

When we live a life of intentional gratitude, we begin to frame how we see our circumstances. I put my favorite photos in frames so I can see them often. They bring me joy as I pass through the room. A smiling five-year-old Steven with his brand-new golden retriever puppy. A strong man-child dressed in a graduation cap and gown. A passel of sun-kissed nieces and nephews standing on the beach with arms on shoulders, windblown hair, and laughing faces. My husband and son wading in the lake at sunset, ready to be baptized together. These are pictures that say, *Remember.*

Gratitude has been called the "memory of the heart."[40] Praise and gratitude bring up pictures in our minds that say, *Remember.*

Isn't that what Jesus did in the last twelve hours of His life as He broke the bread and passed the cup? "And he took bread, gave thanks and broke it, and gave it to them saying, 'This is my body given for you; do this in remembrance of me.' In the same way, after the supper he took the cup" (Luke 22:19–20). Remember. Give thanks.

Glory moments will come and go, sometimes, most times, rather quickly. We must grab hold, savor the moment in the moment, and then remember.

David invites us, "O magnify the LORD with me, and let us exalt His name together" (Psalm 34:3, NASB). When we praise and thank God, we magnify Him—make Him easier to see. A thankful heart opens the windows of heaven that allow us to peek at glory moments all around. Glimpses. Foretastes of our heavenly home that revive our hope and make us hungry for more of Him.

Why does God want us to give thanks and punctuate all of life with gratitude? He knows that gratitude gives birth to joy. Again, it is not what God wants *from* us but what God wants *for* us. Joy. Thanksgiving in "all circumstances" squeezes difficult circumstances until joy oozes out of us. Fruit, if it had a say in the matter, would not like the squeezing, but it is the only way to get the sweet juice past the tough dimpled skin to the outside. Otherwise it would stay locked away until the fruit shriveled up and died.

Perhaps your relationship with God has come to the plateau of routine, passionless religion—as if your faith is stuck on the sandbar of mediocrity when it is truly meant to sail the seas of the joyful life. So what will lift your boat? What will get the joyless you "unstuck"? I suggest the language of a grateful heart will swell the tide to lift your soul from the sandbar and loosen you from the hold of the sucking muck below. Give it a try. As Jonah showed us, the way out of the belly of the whale is praise (see Jonah 2).

When I feel distant from God, gratitude and praise is often the ramp to get me back on the right road. When I have strayed from acknowledging His presence, when I have forgotten *in Him we live and move and have our being,* when I have made myself big and God small, gratitude leads me back to right relationship with Him. And then I wonder why I ever would be so careless as to drift away in the first place.

Earlier I mentioned starting your own *Sudden Glory* journal. In that journal, you can list all that you are grateful for on any given day. After all, realizing and recognizing what God has provided are some of the most resplendent moments of sudden glory you'll experience. Then, on the gray days, when you find yourself in a grumpy mood (come on, I know it happens), pull out your *Sudden Glory* journal and review all the reasons you have to be thankful! I guarantee it will change your perspective and brighten your mood.

Gratitude is the love language of God that enables us to communicate on an intimate level. And if there is one thing that should cause gratitude to bubble up and spill out of our hearts, it is God's grace.

The Amazing Gift of God's Grace

When I turned forty, all of a sudden small letters and numbers got smaller. A trip to the ophthalmologist proved that I needed reading glasses. But I had a hard time keeping track of them, so the doctor fitted me with monovision contact lenses. In my left eye, I wear a contact lens for seeing close up, and in my right eye, I wear a contact lens for seeing farther away. And somehow, my brain figures all that out and I can see clearly.

That is how I view gratitude and grace. With gratitude in one eye and grace in the other, I can see God more clearly.

"What do you think keeps us from experiencing God's grace and true union with Jesus?" my friend Bill asked. "I think it is that we still feel shame, even though we have been exonerated by Christ, forgiven by God, and washed clean by the power of the Holy Spirit," he continued, answering his own question.

[handwritten margin note: SHAME]

And Bill is right. Shame drove Adam and Eve into hiding, and it can drive us there as well. And the only way of escape is to accept God's grace gift and come out into the open. I often find myself crouching in the bushes with Adam and Eve. I hear the footsteps of God approaching the garden in the cool of the evening; He is calling out to me with glory all around, but I cower, naked and ashamed…saddened by how I have failed Him throughout the day.

Sin. It will not cease to exist just because I have entered into this love relationship with Jesus. Yes, I have been saved from the penalty of sin. But the power of sin still pulls my heart toward lesser lovers, and off I go. It tears a drain hole in my soul through which my joy seeps away as I try to soothe that glory ache on my own—apart from Christ. How I long for the day when I leave this earth for the consummation of this heavenly marriage, to be saved from the presence of sin completely. Until then, I fall away again and again, and Jesus woos me back. Grace.

Two of Satan's greatest weapons against Christian women today are shame and condemnation. He knows that because of the finished work of Jesus Christ and His work of redemption in your life, you

[handwritten margin note: I AM]

are deeply loved, completely forgiven, thoroughly cleansed, eternally saved, fully pleasing, and totally accepted by God. All Satan can do is try to convince you it isn't true. He can do nothing to make you un-clean. All he can do is to make you *feel* unclean. And if you believe his lies of shame, then back into the bushes you'll go. Hiding with Adam and Eve as God walks and calls out, "Where are you?"

We all fail God. We all sin. We all fall short of the glory of God, of what He intended us to do and be in the garden. But here's God's promise: "If we confess our sins, he [Jesus] is faithful and just and will forgive us our sins and purify us from all unrighteousness" (1 John 1:9).

What do you do when you fail God? If you're like me, after I have repented and asked forgiveness, my natural tendency is to tell God that I'll try harder next time. Try harder. Is that really the solu-tion? Do I really need to buck it up and try harder? I wonder if that is what Jesus would say.

On the contrary, Jesus said, "If anyone loves me, he will obey my teaching" (John 14:23). Anyone who loves me…will obey my teach-ing. Perhaps the solution to our tendency to disobey God is not trying harder but loving more. Perhaps an intimate relationship with Jesus, one in which we *live and move and have our being in Him* in every aspect of life, is key to obedience. When we love deeply, we are more likely to cling to Him closely.

Jesus has a wonderful way of restoring us when we fail Him. He doesn't humiliate, berate, or criticize us. Rather He takes us aside and asks us to reaffirm our love for Him.

"Do you love me?" Jesus asked Peter three times.

"Yes, Lord, you know that I love you" (John 21:15–17).

No more questions.

It's hard for us to understand. Sometimes grace just doesn't make sense.

THE INVITATION TO FREEDOM THROUGH GRACE

From my inbox:

Dear Sharon,

I just read one of your devotions on receiving grace and forgiveness. You mentioned a woman who had an affair and destroyed her marriage. You said she refused to forgive herself. That really touched me because, you see, eight years ago I had an affair, got pregnant, and had an abortion. This is the first time I have ever actually put those words in writing. I can barely look at what I just typed on the screen.

My marriage was terrible. My husband never paid any attention to me, and we argued all the time. And then a man at work began telling me how pretty I was and how good I smelled. It felt good to be noticed. I knew it was wrong, but I slept with him, and not just once.

Somehow I managed to hide it from my kids and my husband. I even went to church on Sundays, but this sin was eating me alive. No one knew. One day, the stick turned blue. I was pregnant. In order to hide the sin, I had an abortion. I didn't even tell the baby's father. Sin upon sin. I was sin-sick and hated myself.

Not too long after that horrible day, I did turn back to God. I confessed my sin, truly repented, but I've never felt clean. That was eight years ago, and I still can't let go. I wish I could go back and change things. I would willingly give my life to bring this child back. And while I know what the Bible says, that God will forgive us if we confess our sins, I just have a hard time believing it. How could I have done this? How could He forgive me?

Unlike the woman in your devotion, I was a Christian when I had the affair and abortion. I was far from Him at the time, but I did know what I was doing was wrong. My eyes were wide open. I think this is why it is so hard for me to accept God's forgiveness. Sometimes, grace just doesn't make sense. The enemy tells me I'm no good. I think the Holy Spirit is trying to speak to me, but I am having a hard time believing.

How can I forgive myself?

This e-mail comes to me hundreds of times every year. The names are different, the situations are varied, but the underlying theme is the same: *I can't forgive myself. Grace just doesn't make sense. I don't deserve to be forgiven.*

And these women are right…grace doesn't make earthly sense. We don't deserve it. We keep reliving the garden story, choosing Satan's temptations over God's truth, and then grace shows up with an outstretched hand. "I don't deserve it," we cry. And we're right.

Grace, by its very definition, is *unmerited favor from God or a gift we don't deserve.* But until we accept God's grace and forgiveness, Satan will hold us in the vise grip of guilt, and we will miss moments of sudden glory as we hide in Eden's bushes of shame.

After King David's affair with Bathsheba, he was held in the shackles of guilt, unsure if he could ever be set free. But mercy came with the key of forgiveness and flung the prison door open wide. David then had to take the necessary steps to walk out of the prison and into the kingdom of grace.

No matter what you have done, God has made a way for you to be set free—a very costly toll has been paid for the road to your restoration. Jesus gave His life that you might have not only eternal life after physical death but life filled with moments of sudden glory beginning at your spiritual birth.

I in no way want to diminish the seriousness of sin. Neither do I want to lessen the truth of grace. Refusal of the Christian to repent and dogged determination to continue a lifestyle of sin spits in the face of what Christ did on the cross. Unconfessed sin draws the shade on God's glory. Confession with repentance raises the curtain once again for God's glory to shine through.

When we say, "I don't feel forgiven," that is like saying that what Jesus did on the cross is not enough. Why should we require more from ourselves than our Creator requires of us? "Therefore, there is now no condemnation for those who are in Christ Jesus" (Romans 8:1). None. God's grace river washes away the devil's dams of shame and condemnation that block the flow of the glory life.

If you are feeling condemnation for past sins that you have already asked God to forgive, that condemnation is not coming from God. Once you have repented and asked God to forgive you, it is finished, over and done with, wiped away. If feelings of condemnation persist, they are a result of listening to the accusations of the Enemy as he tries to keep you behind those bushes and away from union and communion with God. Believe the truth. Walk in the truth. And it will lead you to moments of sudden glory all around. Without accepting God's grace gift, *in Him we live and move and have our being* will be nigh to impossible to become a reality in your life. A life saturated in grace makes it so.

Satan knows that the slightest whisper of guilt is easily received by a fragile heart, plundered by life. Do not let him convince you to remain in hiding. If you have been crouching in Eden's bushes of shame, listen closely. That sound you hear is God walking your way. Whispering your name. Do you hear it? Singing love songs of grace. Inviting you to stroll with Him in the garden of your heart, where He has taken up permanent residence.

Where are you? I want to commune with you. I want to show you glimpses of My glory. Where are you?

I hope you will say with me, "Here I am, Lord. 'Come, Thou Fount of ev'ry blessing. Tune my heart to sing Thy grace.'"

Focus your lenses of gratitude and grace and embrace the sacred union—the intimate relationship God longs to share with you.

Choosing Intimate Relationship over Routine Religion

> Man's chief end is to glorify God and to
> enjoy him forever.
> —Westminster Shorter Catechism

The glory ache. We all have it. The minute we get that first pop on our tiny bottoms in the delivery room and we inhale the air of this temporary earth, the glory ache is set in motion. Everything we have talked about thus far hinges on this one truth: without a personal relationship with Jesus, the glory ache will persist without real relief. The placebo of religion may mask the inner gnawing, but it will do nothing to ease the hunger pangs of the heart.

Studying God's Word has been one of my greatest joys since the day I became a Christian as a teenager. But sometimes I can get so wrapped up in studying *about* God that I forget my relationship *with* God. I read the Bible, pore through commentaries, and decipher Greek and Hebrew words. However, on many occasions I have allowed my determined mind, which wants to know more *about* God, to override my soul's deepest longing to simply *know God.* All my studying will be stillbirth if I do not move the words from my head to my heart to deepen my relationship with Jesus. If the words do not move me to worship and relationship, then I've missed the point.

[handwritten: This is me.]

All through history there have been men and women who have had an abundance of knowledge about God but have had little to no manifestation of God's presence or power in their lives. Week after week people fill churches to hear well-delivered sermons, only to leave with the glory ache still eating away at their hearts. There is a yearning within our breasts which scholarly teaching simply cannot satisfy.

We can have a right opinion about God. We can agree that He is omnipotent, omnipresent, and omniscient and still not be in right relationship with Him. Satan is proof of that. He knows exactly who God is and what He can do (see James 2:19).

Knowledge about someone will never satisfy the longing to know that person personally. That doesn't mean that we don't study the Bible. But it does mean that we don't stockpile knowledge and miss the intimate relationship Jesus died to make possible. His Word is a means by which He speaks to us *in* relationship. God's Word is not a substitute for the relationship itself.

Jesus warned the religious scholars of his day: "You diligently study the Scriptures because you think that by them you possess eternal life. These are the Scriptures that testify about me, yet you refuse to come to me to have life" (John 5:39–40). Could Jesus be saying the same to me and to you? Have we been filling in the blanks of our well-laid-out Bible study books and neglecting to fill in the blanks of our empty hearts with Him?

We can possess volumes of Bible study knowledge, but if the words do not bring us into a deeper, more intimate relationship with Christ, it becomes of no consequence to us. God's Word may convince us to try harder to be more moral, but head knowledge alone will not transform our lives. It is *to* the heart that God first speaks, and it is *with* the heart that our love relationship grows.

We read what others have learned. We study what teachers have discovered and fill in the blanks of questions they have pondered. We attempt to find intimacy and spiritual depth from predigested truth as we have our seeking done for us. But what about our own questions? What about our own blanks? I certainly have many blanks that need to be filled. When I am in intimate relationship with God, I begin to ask the right questions.

Sound Bible teaching is imperative in our spiritual journey. Without it we would be like children stumbling about in the dark. But knowledge for knowledge's sake will leave us hungry and yearning for something more. The glory ache is never, never satisfied with head knowledge void of application to the heart. It is never mere knowledge that ushers in the glory life, but God Himself. Unless the hearer connects with God on a personal level, she is no better for having heard the words. It is only through relationship—that sacred union—as we *live and move and have our being in Him* that the glory ache will be stayed.

Head Knowledge or Heart Knowledge

If ever there was a group of men who knew the Scriptures, it was the Pharisees and Sadducees of Jesus's day. And yet, time and time again Jesus called them out on their hard hearts. They knew the Scriptures, but they did not know the Scripture Writer. These men had no passion for the God they served. They served out of duty rather than desire, and unfortunately, they passed on their obligatory rule-following religion to the men and women they were supposedly leading to God. Their head knowledge clouded their heart condition. They saw themselves as the best, when in reality, they were to be pitied most of all.

The Pharisees' and Sadducees' cold-hearted efforts to create rule-following clones left soul-hungry people in their wake. Rule-following religion always does. If it could have solved the sin-sickness caused by Eden, then God would have given the Law and left it at that. He didn't.

The Old Testament Law included 613 rules and regulations added to the Ten Commandments. I don't know how the people were expected to remember them, much less keep them. But Jesus challenged the Pharisees' pious traditions and condemned them for not practicing what they preached. He called them out for making a big show to be noticed by men, for elevating themselves with titles, and for overlooking their hardness of heart. They were the most religious men of their day, and yet they were void of any relationship with God. Their hearts were far from Him.

> Then some Pharisees and teachers of the law came to Jesus from Jerusalem and asked, "Why do your disciples break the tradition of the elders? They don't wash their hands before they eat!"

Jesus replied, "And why do you break the command of
God for the sake of your tradition?... Thus you nullify the
word of God for the sake of your tradition. You hypocrites!
Isaiah was right when he prophesied about you:
'These people honor me with their lips,

but their hearts are far from me.
They worship me in vain;

their teachings are but rules taught by men.'"
        (Matthew 15:1–3, 6–9)

Paul, on the other hand, a Pharisee lawman turned Christ-following
grace-man, longed to know God intimately. He was willing to give up
everything to experience the divine romance and sacred union. He
wrote:

What is more, I consider everything a loss compared to the sur-
passing greatness of knowing Christ Jesus my Lord, for whose
sake I have lost all things.... *I want to know Christ* and the power
of his resurrection and the fellowship of sharing in his sufferings,
becoming like him in his death, and so, somehow, to attain to the
resurrection from the dead. (Philippians 3:8, 10–11)

Saul, the Pharisee who had been perfectly content knowing the
facts about God, became Paul, the Christian who was willing to give up
everything to know the heart of God. He wanted to know Jesus personally and experientially. And while God longs to have a relationship with
His children, He waits to be wanted.

Paul wanted that love relationship for himself, and he wanted it for you. This was his prayer for you.

> I pray that you, being rooted and established in love, may have power, together with all the saints, to *grasp* how wide and long and high and deep is the love of Christ, and to know this love that surpasses knowledge—that you may be filled to the measure of all the fullness of God. (Ephesians 3:17–19)

Paul prayed that you would be rooted like a tree firmly fixed with deep roots, able to withstand the storms and droughts of life. He also prayed that you would be firmly established in God's love like a building with a strong foundation that will not move with shifting times. And he prayed that you would know...oh, that you would know.

Notice Paul used the words *know* and *knowledge*. The first word, *know,* is *gnosis* or *ginosko.* This word encompasses a very personal level of familiarity and was often used to describe the intimate relationship between a husband and a wife. This word is not simply a head knowledge but an intimate heart knowledge.

The word he used for "knowledge" is a little different than the Greek word *gnosis.* It is more of a head knowledge, an intellectual reckoning. Paul was praying that you would *know by experience* what you *know in your head.* That type of knowing comes through glory moments when you experience God as you *live and move and have your being in Him.* You don't get that by studying alone. You get that by experiencing God through an intimate relationship.

Paul really wanted us to "get it" when it came to understanding

God's love for us and His desire for intimacy. "I pray that you may grasp…" It almost sounds like a pleading. "Come on, friend," he might have said. "You've got to get this. You've got to grab hold of this truth. This is not about having a religion in your life. I had a religion and I was the most miserable man alive. This is about having a relationship with Christ. This is important!"

The Greek word for "grasp" is *katalamana* and means "to lay hold of, seize with eagerness, suddenness…"[41] Suddenness! I love that word. I can almost hear God saying, "Surprise! This is just for you! Lay hold of it! A sudden glory!"

When moments of sudden glory occur, when you catch a glimpse of just how much God loves you, then grab hold. Grasp the moments. Seize them with eagerness. Don't let go.

The glory ache within all of us will not be soothed with theological studies, even though those studies may well pave the way. During difficult times, even the best theology can fail you if it isn't accompanied by experience bathed in relationship. The glory ache will be stayed by experiencing intimacy with God as He speaks to your heart and reveals His presence—His glory.

How many thirsty people are reading about the source to quench all thirst and yet remain on the water's edge without dipping in their cups to take a drink? A beautiful lake sits just a few steps from my back door. I can gaze at the lake, stare in awe of the lake, and even stand in the lake. But I will die of thirst if I do not lift the water to my lips and drink. Likewise, we can read about God, stand in awe of God, and even attend church on a regular basis. But if we do not dip our cups into the well of His heart and drink, if we do not enter into intimacy with Him, the thirst will go unquenched.

So why study the Bible? One reason is to know God better. If it seems I've gone in a circle, it is because in a way I have. We study to find out more about God. We spend time with Him to know Him intimately, personally, deeply.

I don't want another lesson. I want to taste, to see, to hear, to touch, to sense God's presence. I want more than to hear a good lesson and say, "That was good." I want to experience God and say, "He is good!"

PRACTICING RELIGION OR ENJOYING RELATIONSHIP

When I was a little girl, I loved pretending to be a bride. I'd wrap a sheet around my body, drape a towel over my head, and hold a bouquet of plastic flowers to my chest. Then I would start at one end of the hallway in our ranch-style house and saunter down the "aisle." In my little mind, all eyes were on me as my sheet became a pearl-studded wedding gown, my towel a lace veil, and the bouquet a spray of white roses.

My uncle Ernest understood the longings of little girls to be brides, so for Christmas one year he gave me a two-foot-tall doll dressed in full bridal regalia. Along with her white wedding gown and netlike veil, she had cropped, curly brown hair that felt as real as my own, soft plump skin that squished when I squeezed her, and moveable eyelids lined with thick black lashes. Her eyes opened and closed with her changing positions so that when she lay in her box, she resembled Sleeping Beauty just waiting to be kissed. Her perfectly shaped lips were small and dainty, and her crystal-blue eyes appeared strangely real.

But there was one problem with this delightful gift. Because she was so expensive, my mother wouldn't allow me to play with her.

"You'll have to wait until you are older," she explained. "She's too nice to play with. You might tear her gown. We'll just keep her in the box until you're old enough to know how to take care of her."

So the bride doll remained in her box, safely stowed away in the bottom dresser drawer. Day after day, I slowly opened the drawer and stole a peek at my doll as she lay sleeping inside the drawer like a treasure in a safety deposit box. Sometimes I removed the box lid and gently stroked her pink skin, but I knew if I ever took her out of the box and played with her, I would be in big trouble. As time passed, I forgot about the bride doll in the drawer, and today, I don't even know what became of her.

I am sure the doll's fate was never my uncle's intent when he gave her to me. I imagine he envisioned me spending hours and hours playing with her, pretending with her, and enjoying her. As a matter-of-fact, had he known the doll lived in the bottom dresser drawer, I think he would have been sorely disappointed.

Oh, friend, have we done the same with the greatest gift of all time—Jesus? Have we accepted the gift of the gospel and then stored it away in a drawer for safekeeping? Have we put Jesus on display but neglected or refused to enjoy Him? Have we made the gospel into a religion in a box rather than a relationship in the heart?

As quoted at the start of the chapter, the Shorter Catechism of the Westminster Confession of Faith, written by the Westminster Assembly of 1646, states, "Man's chief end is to *glorify* God and to *enjoy* him forever" (emphasis mine). Enjoy God! The only way to enjoy God is by being in His presence, by making Acts 17:28, "In him we live and move and have our being," a present reality. Glory moments will not be found in a boxed-up religion but in a budding relationship.

What does God want from us? Some say that He wants obedience and sacrifice—that He wants us to stick to the rule book and color inside the lines. Others say that God wants us to be happy and victorious in all things. None of that is necessarily wrong, but it is not the greatest desire of God's heart. What He longs for, more than anything, is for you to be in relationship with Him. He wants your heart. He wants you to enjoy Him, to love Him, to join Him in intimacy as *you live and move and have your being in Him.*

WORK OR WORSHIP

In our culture, the desire to *feel* closer to God causes Christians to ramp up their church attendance, join humanitarian causes, and cough up cash for the needy. People yearn for something more, and they aren't even sure what that something more is, so they grasp at one possible solution and then another.

Religion or its disciplines will never satisfy the nagging glory ache of the heart. The adherence to doctrines, a devotion to disciplines, or compliance to a spit-shined compilation of dos and don'ts will not satisfy the longing. While all of those activities may be advantageous to the soul, they are intended to enhance our love relationship with Jesus, never to replace it.

God created us to glorify Him, to respond to Him, to walk in union with Him.

God the Father, God the Son, and God the Holy Spirit exist in triune relationship—union—with each other. You were created in

God's image for the same purpose—to exist in relationship with the Trinity, *to live and move and have your being in Him.*

We were made for relationship. That is why we crave it so passionately. We can ignore God's wooing and seek satisfaction in earthly relationships, but they will always leave us with a gnawing hunger for something more. No relationship will satisfy the glory ache except one with the King of glory Himself.

For many, the relationship that God intended has degenerated into religion filled with meetings, checklists, and good works—as if business translates into godliness. Sunday morning worship becomes part of a routine habit that is endured rather than a celebration in which God's children come together in corporate worship. The offering plate has become a way to ease guilt or appease God rather than a way to express our love to Him. The words of Scripture saunter into our minds, kicking up nothing but a little intellectual dust rather than moving our hearts to deeper intimacy. If we allow ourselves to get caught up in the whirlwind of Christian duty, the romance may very well be whisked away.

Religious activity apart from an intimate relationship with God is empty ritual. Empty. Unfortunately, we can become so comfortable practicing religion that we don't even recognize the absence of relationship. That's certainly what happened to the religious leaders of Jesus's day. That can happen so easily to you and to me.

Jesus warned the disciples to beware of the yeast or the influence of the Pharisees and Sadducees (see Matthew 16:6). He told the crowd, "The teachers of the law and the Pharisees sit in Moses's seat. So you must obey them and do everything they tell you. But do not do what they do, for they do not practice what they preach. They *tie up heavy loads and put them on men's shoulders,* but they themselves are not willing to lift a finger to move them. Everything they do is done for men to see" (Matthew 23:2–5).

These words were in stark contrast to Jesus's words, "Take my yoke upon you and learn from me.... For my yoke is easy and my burden is light" (Matthew 11:29–30). Again, we've made our relationship with Jesus far too difficult and complicated. It's just not that hard. He never intended it to be.

Jesus went on to point out the hollowness, futility, and vanity of the Pharisees' religious practices: they gave a tenth of their spices but were neglectful of justice, mercy, and faithfulness; they cleaned the outside of their cups but left the inside of their hearts full of greed; they looked pristine on the outside but were like empty tombs on the inside; they honored the prophets of old when men just like the Pharisees had been the ones who killed them. Jesus spurned the practices that the religious leaders thought were most important.

The religious leaders condemned Jesus for eating with tax collectors and sinners, healing the sick on the Sabbath, and for allowing a repentant woman to wash His feet with her salty tears. Jesus's harshest words were not directed at the sinners who gathered to hear Him speak but at the religious leaders who paraded about with their law-loving, pious, pickle-faced noses in the air. It seemed the men and women that the religious folks called "sinners" were the very ones who understood who Jesus was and what He came to do. They were the ones that "got it."

Jesus did not give His life to make us more moral. He didn't die on that cruel Roman cross, have thorns pressed into His forehead and a spear thrust into his side so that we could be happy little people who go to church on Sundays, read our Bibles every now and then, use good manners in society, and support local charities. He did not leave His eternal throne in heaven, walk this earth dressed in the confines of human flesh, and endure rejection as men spat in His face so that we could prosper financially and live free of suffering. Oh my, how these words sting my heart. As I consider how we have watered down the Christian life and dressed it up in our Sunday best, I pray for forgiveness. I pray for mercy. For it is not only the Pharisees who chose religion over relationship, it is often the twenty-first-century church as well.

It is easy for us to fall into the trap of reading about the Pharisees and immediately agreeing that they were the bad guys. But we've got to get this. These were the religious rulers, the church folks.

We would be remiss not to stop and observe our own actions in the mirror of Jesus's words. Are we religious? What would Jesus have said to you and to me had we been standing in the courtyard that day?

When you have a religion in your life rather than a relationship, that glory ache will not be satisfied. At some point renewed religious activity will serve no purpose except to make you feel a little better about yourself.

Impressing People or Blessing God

Religion can be very self-serving rather than God honoring. I fear many of our religious practices are meant to impress each other rather than honor God. The desire to shine makes us want to appear better than we are. The fear that we will be found out pushes us to doctor up our spiritual resumes. I dare say that those who adhere to a "works doctrine," as we have come to call it, are more interested in what others think than what God knows.

Sometimes we choose religious duty over obedience to God. Do you find it difficult to distinguish the two? There's only one way: by determining relationship (or lack of it). In Mark 1:35, we see Jesus rising early in the morning and going away to a quiet place to commune with His heavenly Father—just the two of them. After a few moments, His disciples came looking for Him, explaining that the people in the village wanted Him to come back and heal more people. Jesus said no.

"Let us go somewhere else—to the nearby villages—so I can preach there also. That is why I have come" (verse 38).

When we *live and move and have our being* in Jesus, when we enter into God's continual conversation and listen to Him, we will know when to say yes and when to say no. The *need* is not the *call.* I cannot tell you how many times I have had to repeat that one sentence to myself. We must choose obedience to God over religious duty lest we miss moments of sudden glory because we're too busy doing something God never intended for us to do in the first place.

I do get weary of religion that has absolutely nothing to do with Jesus. It's as if I am standing in the courtyard while Jesus turns over the moneychangers' tables and wondering if He will come to my table next.

Some of the most unhappy people I know are very religious, and honestly, I try to steer clear of them. Jesus said, "Be especially careful when you are trying to be good so that you don't make a performance out of it. It might be good theater, but the God who made you won't be applauding" (Matthew 6:1, MSG).

We are drawn to personal relationship with God, and yet we fear it. It's unpredictable and somewhat mystical. Scripture memorization, Bible study classes, scheduled quiet times, church attendance, and tithing 10 percent are all easy to control. Relationship is not.

Saul was a very religious man. We meet him in Acts chapter 7, keeping watch over the clothes of the men and women who stoned Stephen to death. May I say that again? Saul was religious. Very religious. He was a Pharisee who wore the right religious clothes, used the right religious lingo, and studied under the smartest religious teachers. And he worked, worked, worked, for God. What a guy!

But then he had an encounter. On the road. On the way to do some more work for God. Saul was on his way to Damascus with papers from the high priest giving permission to arrest more followers of Jesus known as "the Way." And whom should Mr. Religious meet on the road to Damascus but Jesus Himself.

Saul was blinded by the Light and confronted by the Truth: "Saul, Saul, why are you persecuting me?" (see Acts 9:1–5). It is no wonder that Saul, who was later known as Paul, would one day write to the Ephesians and tell them he was praying that God would open the eyes of their hearts (1:18–19). *I am asking God to open the eyes of my heart*

Oh, that we, like Paul, would come to a halt in our religious routine and meet Jesus along the way. That we, like Paul, would learn to *live and move and have our being* in the One who opens eyes to see God's glory all around.

DUTY OR DESIRE

My ministry is primarily with women, and often the subject of marriage comes up. And for those brave souls who dare ask the hard questions, sex surfaces as one of the top three areas of marital tension. Questions brim from frustration, and sometimes my answers are not what they want to hear. Frequency? Foreplay? What is acceptable and unacceptable? What is required?

Required? Do women really ask that? Yes. *Required.* That's the word they use. Far too many women, Christians included, approach the marriage bed with a sense of duty rather than the sensuality of desire. And you know what? A husband always knows the difference. He can tell when his wife is enduring the process rather than enjoying the passion. And while he may feel a sense of release when the song is sung, it is not the melody his heart longs for—a song in which his wife desires him, enjoys him, and looks forward to moments of intimacy with him. *I want to get to this point!*

And guess what? God knows the difference too. I'm not talking about sexual intimacy here. I'm talking about spiritual intimacy. God can tell when we are serving Him out of duty and when we are serving Him out of an overflow of our great love. He knows when our time with Him is simply a number on our to-do list and when it is our heart's greatest desire.

We dutifully work and we strive and we study and we push and we push and we push. If we stop all this bustling about to become good Christians, we just might fall in love with Jesus all over again.

David sang, "In your presence is fullness of joy" (Psalm 16:11, NKJV). The Hebrew word for "joy" used here is *simchah* and means "glee, gladness, intense joy, pleasure, rejoicing, an outward expression."[42] It is not simply an outward emotion but an inner state of being.

Serving God out of duty will leave you drained emotionally and spiritually. Serving God out of desire may leave you tired physically, but you will not be drained. Sometimes serving God out of desire, out of the overflow of a relationship with Him, can make you downright giddy.

Peter wrote: "Though you have not seen him, you love him; and even though you do not see him now, you believe in him and are filled with an *inexpressible and glorious joy,* for you are receiving the goal of your faith, the salvation of your souls" (1 Peter 1:8–9). Inexpressible joy! We can't even describe it with words. Glorious joy! Joy that is full of heaven and a reflection of the very face of God. Even in our most difficult circumstances, we can still experience "inexpressible and glorious joy."

The word *joy* comes from a word that means "making merry." I am taken back to C. S. Lewis's musing that Christians lack "merriment." Could it be that one of the reasons we lack merriment, or joy, is that we are not acknowledging His presence *as we live and move and have our being* in Christ? Could it be that we think we are on this journey basically alone with little visits from God every now and then?

Our freedom, our passion, our joy that spills out from intimacy with God will unnerve those confined by the limits of law and driven by duty. They may attempt to rein us in, calm us down, and shush our praise. Some call the stilling of expressive worship reverence. I call it sad.

The stodgy churchgoer looks on with distain as the winsome worshipper raises her hands and sings with reckless abandon. But I wonder if the observer secretly longs for that same freedom in her heart of hearts? *What if?* she muses before common sense pushes the wonderings aside.

The world is watching. Is there a scowl on your brow that makes others turn away because the Christian life appears too hard? Or is there a smile on your face that stirs others to want to join the family?

Making a Change

If you realize your Christian faith has been more of a religion than a relationship, it's not too late to change! Like a toddler's unsteady first steps, it may feel a bit uncomfortable at first. Yes, relationship is less predictable than religion, but until one makes the change, a hollow emptiness will prevail. And once you step into an intimate relationship with Jesus, that joy you've always longed for will begin to flow.

Look at the difference it made in Pam's life:

Dear Sharon:

I am writing to let you know how much your online devotion meant to me today. Your journey to intimacy with God is very similar to what God has been showing me over this past year. I have been a Christian for thirty-one years, but thirty of those years I spent performing to get God's approval. I believed the lie that God's love was somehow dependent upon what I did or didn't do. Up until this year, if you had asked me to describe my Christian life, I would have said that I am saved but empty. I did not see God as a loving heavenly Father and I as His precious daughter. I saw Him as a stern judge with arms crossed and a scowl on his face. I felt more condemned than accepted. I imagined disappointment in His eyes instead of delight when He looked at me.

I was not raised in a Christian home...far from it. When I

was fourteen, I accepted Christ. I wanted to know how to live the Christian life. I actually thought there was a list in a pastor's file somewhere that would tell me what I should and should not do. I soon learned there was no such list, so I did the next best thing I could think of. I paid attention to other Christians. If they said Christians did not do certain things, those "things" went on my list. I spent thirty years adding to the list, rarely taking anything off. As you can imagine, the list grew quite long. God did show me that some things were right or wrong, but most of what I believed came from what church people said. What started out as a sincere desire to live the Christian life became bondage to a legalistic mind-set.

From the outside, I looked pretty good. I graduated from Bible college, taught in Christian schools, married a Christian man, bore three children who became Christians, and I was very involved in church work. But my daily, personal life was empty. I didn't have a hunger for God's Word, and I rarely heard Him speak to me in a personal way. Prayer was touch and go. I knew Christ as Savior, but somehow I could not connect with Him in a deep, personal way.

It wasn't until last February that God began to show me there was a better way to live my Christian life. He was probably trying to show me before, but I wasn't paying attention. Now I was. As I read the Bible, He began showing me just how He felt about me—His opinion of me. I began praying conversationally with Him rather than repeating rote prayers or reading down a list.

Once I discovered that God loves me unconditionally and that He wants to have a relationship with me, I began to serve Him out of the overflow of a full heart rather than out of fear or duty. Now I feel free in several areas of my life…areas that have brought so much joy. I feel free to read the Bible from various versions rather than just the King James. I feel free to listen to contemporary Christian music that draws me into His presence like never before. (I have twenty years of contemporary Christian music to catch up on!) And the denominational walls that I had built came tumbling down. Having a relationship with Jesus rather than a religion has opened my life up to fellowshiping with people from all denominations.

God has been taking me through a process of dismantling religious "boxes," which He never intended for me to build or crawl into. I can honestly say that I am not the same person I was one year ago.

—Pam

Isn't that what you want too? To experience that intimate personal relationship with the Lover of your soul? To taste and see that the Lord is good? When we exchange routine religion for intimate relationship with Jesus, we will say with Pam, "I can honestly say I am not the same person I was before."

A sudden glory!

From Glory to Glory

> If I find in myself a desire which no
> experience in the world can satisfy, the most
> probable explanation is that I was made for
> another world.
>
> —C. S. Lewis, *Mere Christianity*

I grew up in a lovely Southern neighborhood in eastern North Carolina. Our home was a traditional brick ranch-style with columns supporting the front porch and sixty-foot-tall pine trees forming a shady canopy above. A bountiful palette of pink, purple, and fuchsia azaleas wreathed the immaculate yard in the spring, and long-needle pine straw rained down in the fall. The welcoming red door on the house portrayed the picture of tranquility and peace, but inside the walls teemed with an atmosphere of hostility and fear.

My father was a businessman who was away most of the time.

When he was home, he had bouts of heavy drinking followed by violent fits of rage. My parents fought both verbally and physically, and their wide-eyed, terrified children saw it all. Heated arguments, black eyes, and broken furniture were common occurrences. I remember going to bed at night, pulling the covers tightly around my chin and praying that I would hurry and fall asleep to shut out the noise of the screaming and yelling in the next room. Occasionally, I crept out of bed, tiptoed over to my little pink jewelry box nestled on my dresser, and turned a silver key in the back. When fully cranked, I opened the lid and listened to the fairylike music playing as a ballerina turned with hands overhead. With eyes squeezed shut, I pretended I was that tiny dancer in a faraway place where there was no screaming…where there was no fear.

The mornings following the eruptions were always the same. My mother moved about the house in angry silence, and my father cried and begged for forgiveness. He swore the drunken rage, the hitting, and the yelling would never happen again. But it did.

Amazingly, as miserable as we were, my family went to church on Sundays. I dreaded Saturday nights, when my mother wound my hair on what seemed like a million tiny, pink sponge curlers. It seemed I could never find a comfortable place to lay my head on the pillow where the curlers didn't pull at my scalp.

The next morning, we'd rush about, put on our Sunday best, and drive dutifully to the doors of the church in silence. Most of the time my parents were mad about something; at least that's how it seemed to me. But by golly, we were going to church…lookin' good.

"How are you today?" other well-dressed members would say.

"Fine, and you?" we all dutifully replied. But we were anything but fine, and I suspect many of the pristine families sitting in the shiny pews around us weren't either.

When I was twelve years old, I joined the church after a six-week confirmation class and was baptized to "seal the deal." But as the pastor dipped me under the water and then raised me up "to newness of life," as he stated, I was no more a new creation than Jane Doe buried in the local cemetery. I was more concerned with my hair getting wet than with my eternal soul. The following Sunday, I walked across the stage in my crisp, white dress and received a pin and certificate to commemorate the occasion. It was official: I now had religion.

But God...oh, but God. But God didn't leave me that way. Religion was not His goal for this gal. That's not what He had in mind.

Shortly after getting my pin and paper for church membership, a friend's mother took special interest in me. The Hendersons lived two blocks from our house, and Wanda, their red-headed daughter, and I began to spend a lot of time together. I loved being in the Hendersons' home. It was filled with joy, laughter, and lots of love. For the first time, I saw a relationship between a husband and wife the way God intended. In my adolescent mind, I didn't know why that family was so different than mine, but I knew it had something to do with Jesus.

Mrs. Henderson sang about Jesus, talked about Jesus, and seemed to move about the house as if she were arm-in-arm with Him. And the strangest thing (I did think it strange) was that this woman talked about Jesus and to Jesus like she knew Him personally. She talked about Him like they were best friends.

The Hendersons loved church. That was also something new for me. I'd never known anyone who really *loved* church. It was just something that good people did each week. Visit the dentist twice a year, rotate your tires every five thousand miles, and go to church once a week. But to actually *love* church or look forward to going? That was a foreign concept.

Eventually, I began going to church with the Hendersons, and I discovered a whole bunch of folks who talked *to* Jesus and *about* Jesus like they knew Him personally. I listened to the pastor teach from the Bible, the choir sing from their hearts, and the congregation praise God from grateful souls. When they prayed, there were no *thees* and *thous*. They spoke to God as if they were speaking to a beloved friend or a caring father.

For two years I observed these people who showed me the difference between having a Sunday morning religion and having an everyday relationship with Jesus. I saw them as they *lived and moved and had their being in Him*. I listened to them tell stories of sudden glory as God made Himself visible in their lives.

"Let me tell you what God showed me yesterday in Scripture," one of them would say.

"Listen to what God did in my life on Thursday," another would exclaim.

"God gave me an amazing picture of just how much He loves me," another would chime in.

Though I didn't know what to call it then, I felt the glory ache when I heard them talk like this. I wanted what they had. Then one night, when I was fourteen years old, Mrs. Henderson sat me down on her den sofa and asked, "Sharon, are you ready to receive Jesus as your Lord and Savior?"

With tears streaming down my cheeks, I said yes.

And that, my friend, was the beginning of the great adventure and my most magnificent sudden glory moment of all. Salvation was not the end of God's redemptive journey for me; it was only the beginning. And over the next six years, through many twists and turns that only God's hand could have orchestrated, both of my parents came to Christ as well.

Interestingly, though the glory ache subsided the night I said yes to Him, it didn't go away altogether. It lingered, and I wondered why.

Not Home Yet

Do you ever feel like you are not at home here on earth? That even with Christ in your life something is still missing? The reason is because you're *not* at home, and something *is* missing. C. S. Lewis wrote in *Mere Christianity,* "If I find in myself a desire which no experience in this world can satisfy, the most probable explanation is that I was made for another world."

Solomon reminds us, "He [God] has planted eternity in the human heart" (Ecclesiastes 3:11, NLT). You were made for eternity, for glory, and as long as your feet are here on this earth, you will experience a glory ache that only heaven can fully satisfy. You will feel a certain something missing that may be hard to define.

One spring, our family hosted a ten-year-old Russian foreign exchange student. He went to school with my son and got a taste of what the American Christian family is all about. Alex's English was very limited, and we depended on hand signals and facial expressions to get by.

On one occasion, I was trying to get him to write a letter to his parents. I pulled out the stationery, handed him a pen, and pointed to a picture of his mother and father. "Why don't you write a letter to your parents?" I suggested. He had no idea what I was talking about.

For twenty minutes I drew pictures and tried to get him to understand what I wanted him to do. Finally, with tears in his eyes, he looked up at me and said, "What do?"

I just hugged him and put the pen and paper away.

Oftentimes I feel like our little foreign exchange student. I see beauty mingled with pain and suffering and wonder…*What do?* I feel close to God but not close enough, and I cry…*What do?* I see glimpses of God's presence, but the ache never quite goes completely away, and I look toward heaven and pray…*What do?*

Then God reminds me that I am not home yet. I am an alien and a stranger in this world in which I temporarily live (1 Peter 2:11; Hebrews 11:13). My citizenship, your citizenship, is in heaven (Philippians 3:20), and we are just passing through this wonderful, very fleeting point in time and space we call life. There will always be a tension between the physical world and our new born-again spirit that was made for eternity.

Another translation of Ecclesiastes 3:11 reads, "He also has planted eternity in men's hearts and minds [a divinely implanted sense of a purpose working through the ages which nothing under the sun but God alone can satisfy]" (AMP). Not until we see Jesus face to face will the lingering glory ache completely subside. I can almost hear the collective "ahhhh" that is sure to come when we believers exhale our last earthly breath and inhale eternity for the first time.

Our culture has made very little of heaven and tried desperately to create heaven here on earth. Advertisers bank on the idea that people really think this is as good as it gets. Modern man engages in ceaseless activity and amusement to distract himself from considering what comes next. Even the prayer life of Christians shows just how little we think of heaven. We spend more time praying for believers to be healed (which keeps them out of heaven) than we do praying for unbelievers to be saved (which could keep them out of hell).

For years I read 1 Corinthians 2:9 and wondered just what God had planned for me here on earth. "No eye has seen, no ear has heard, no mind has conceived what God has prepared for those who love him." My nearsightedness kept these words earthbound. Not once did I consider that God could have been speaking of all that He has planned for me in eternity...until now. But through this study of God's lavish response to our ache for something more, I have come to realize that total healing of the glory ache will come when I finally make it home. The door upon which I have been knocking all my life will finally swing open when I step into eternity.

The glory ache will not be satisfied by working harder or by doing more but by living a life of sacred union in which Acts 17:28 becomes a practical and perpetual reality in your life. The glory ache can be soothed by erasing the lines that separate the sacred from the secular so that every endeavor becomes an act of worship. By joining God's continual conversation as He pursues you, romances you, and speaks to you first one way and then another. By daring to raise your expectations and entering into His world. By taking His hand and joining Him in the divine dance of obedience where you follow His lead in a unique choreography designed just for you. By opening the windows of heaven through words of gratitude and grace. In each of these venues, God softly announces His presence through shimmering hues of radiance, tapping gently at your consciousnesses and seeking entrance into the moments of your day.

But even then…the glory ache will not go away completely, for we see as through a glass dimly. The dull throb of "homesickness" will remain until we see Him face to face and experience the joy of His presence in unrestricted ecstasy. Until then, God gives us glimpses of glory here on earth.

Glimpses, they come and they go. The choir stops. The sunset fades. The rose drops its petals. The kiss ceases. Thunder quiets. The wind stills. The stars disappear in the morning light. We want to live in a constant state of awe, but we can't. Our human limitations won't allow it. Our minds, our bodies, our emotions couldn't contain it. The circuitry of our humanness would overload.

So I stand in the cleft of the rock with Moses as God holds His hand over my face, and allows me to look at His back as His glory passes by (Exodus 33:18–23). How I thank Him for moments of sudden glory that tide me over until I'm finally home.

CAPTIVATED BY GLORY

My friends Gwen, Lisa, and Bill joined Steve and me for a shrimp boil at my home. We spread out the steamed shrimp and then made a glorious mess as we shucked and ate one tasty morsel after another.

After dinner Gwen and I challenged Bill and Lisa to a paddle boat race across the lake. "Oh, we'll cream you guys," Bill boasted as he and his paddling partner accepted the challenge. He puffed up, knowing that victory was imminent. He was pumped.

I pointed Bill toward one of our two vessels. "Here, you take this one."

"Fine with me," he said, self-assured.

My husband, with a knowing smile, signaled for the race to begin. Off we went. Bill and Lisa paddled furiously and pulled out ahead. While Bill had his eye on the finish line across the lake, I turned around in my seat and lowered our secret weapon. Unbeknownst to Bill, our boat had a silent, hidden, battery-powered bass motor. I dropped the motor, flipped the switch, and in no time we passed our competitors and left them in our tiny wake. While Bill and Lisa paddled frantically like milkmaids churning butter, Gwen and I sliced through the water like a hot knife through cream.

Bill was confused. We were tickled.

Of course, Gwen and I won the race. We made it to the opposite shore in half the time of our confused competitors. As we turned the boat around and headed back toward a befuddled Bill, I called out. "Oh, I forgot to mention that our boat has a battery-powered motor!"

He headed right toward us and splashed us in good fashion.

Gwen and I paddled back to home base, but Bill and Lisa stayed in the middle of the lake as the sun began to sink and streak the evening sky with the handiwork of God. Orange, magenta, and red filled the heavenly expanse. Geese conversed. Crickets chirped. Cicadas sang. Deep-throated frogs gave bass notes to nature's melody. The moon rose and reflected its face in the water as the mass of summer musicians celebrated the season. And right smack-dab in the middle of the lake sat two of God's children, awestruck. Captivated. And you know what? I was captivated by watching their response to God's glory.

Isn't that the way of glory? As we see others *living and moving and having their being in Jesus,* we want it too. As we sense their sacred inloveness, we long for the same passionate intimacy with God in our own lives. Don't be surprised if your moments of sudden glory cause others to tug on your shirtsleeve with hungry eyes and want to know more. Tell them! Oh, how I pray that you will tell them! Tell them of the moments of sudden glory that brim in a woman's heart when she *lives and moves and has her being in Christ.* Tell them of glory moments strewn about by God's willing hand for eyes to see, ears to hear, hearts to embrace. What an amazing truth: God uses me and you to open hungry eyes to recognize His presence all around—to glorify Him— to make His presence known.

A sudden glory!

A Sudden Glory—

Your Journaling Space

STUDY GUIDE

The following lessons are designed to lead you into a deeper understanding and more intimate relationship with Jesus. I invite you to pull up to God's banquet table, open the feast of His Word, and taste and see that He is good! Whether you are doing this study in a group or on your own, I pray that you will have many moments of sudden glory as God shows you just how much He loves you and longs to be a part of every moment of your day!

Lesson 1: The Glory Ache

We all come into this world with a longing for something more than this earth could ever give. Let's begin our journey by taking a look at how others who have gone before us tried to satisfy their glory ache.

1. How did the following people describe their glory ache?

   Isaiah 26:9

   Psalm 42:1–2

   Psalm 63:1

   Psalm 84:2

2. Read and record Isaiah 55:1–2. Can you give some examples of things we labor for or search for that will not satisfy our heart's glory ache?

3. The Hebrew word for "satisfy" is *saba* and means "to have enough, be full…sufficiency."[43] Have you ever worked for or longed for something you thought would bring satisfaction, but when you got it, you discovered it didn't fill that void in your heart after all? If so, describe what happened.

4. Jeremiah speaks much about the Israelites who turned to idol worship to satisfy their glory ache rather than to God. Read Jeremiah 2:11–13. Jeremiah said the people had made cisterns that could not hold water. How is a broken or cracked cistern representative of anything we would use to fill the glory ache other than a relationship with Jesus?

5. Read John 4:13–14. What did Jesus say He came to give?

The NIV Study Bible describes the phrase *welling up* in verse 14 as a vigorous expression with a meaning like "leaping up." Jesus was speaking of vigorous, abundant life that comes with intimate relationship (see John 10:10). He offers not just to quench your thirst today but offers but a continual stream that flows through your life as you *live and move and have your being in Him.*

Compare and contrast the living water welling up from within your heart with the broken cisterns Jeremiah described.

6. In John 7:37–38 what is His invitation to us all?

7. Read and record Jeremiah 31:25. The Hebrew word for "faint" is *da'ab* and means "to pine." How are the glory ache and "to pine" similar? You may want to look up *pine* in a dictionary.

What happens when we *pine* for something or someone? Have you ever felt a pining for something you couldn't quite identify? Describe what you felt or thought.

8. How did David pray for God to satisfy his glory ache?

     Psalm 90:14

     Psalm 63:1–3

     Psalm 63:4

9. Let's end today by praying that God will fill us up. Pray that He will soothe the glory ache in our hearts and that we won't be so foolish as to look for someone else or something else to do what only He can do.

10. If you are working through these lessons with a group, share what you hope to take away at the end of this study. If you are working independently, jot down what you hope to learn.

Lesson 2: Recognizing God's Passionate Pursuit

God always makes the first move in the passionate pursuit of the human heart. Let's take a look at the lengths He will go through to woo and win you.

1. *Chesed* is a Hebrew word used for God's unfailing love throughout the Old Testament. It is always used of God, not of humans. He alone can give that type of love. What does Psalm 136 tell you about God's love?

2. What does Jeremiah 31:3 tell you about God's love for you? What picture do the words "drawn you" paint in your mind?

3. Religion is about man reaching up to God, but the gospel is about God reaching down to man. Read Psalm 18:16–19. How did David say that God pursued and rescued him?

   For the writers of the Psalms, the sea was a symbol of threatening forces or circumstances. How did God reach down and pluck you from the most threatening force of all? Why did He do this?

4. Read Isaiah 62:5, 12. How does Isaiah describe God's delight over you? How does he describe the people who God pursued and won?

God doesn't just delight over you with a smile. According to Zephaniah 3:17, what else does He do to show His delight?

Read and record Song of Songs 7:10. What does this verse stir in your heart?

5. Let's look at how God pursued one particular woman's heart. Read John 4:1–26. Jesus didn't "have to" go through Samaria because of proximity. When a Jew's travels took him near Samaria, he actually crossed over the Jordan River, went around Samaria, and then crossed over the Jordan again to get back on the road. He took this longer route to avoid the Samaritans, whom the Jews despised.

So why did Jesus "have to" go through Samaria? (See John 5:30; 6:38; 8:26.)

Where were the disciples?

Why do you think Jesus stayed by the well and sent the disciples to get food?

Who showed up? What does the passage reveal about her life?

This was the longest recorded conversation between Jesus and any one person in the New Testament. It was also the first time He told someone his true identity...that He was the Messiah. He did all this in a culture in which women were not allowed to talk to men in public, a Jew was not allowed to drink from a Samaritan's cup, and a woman was not allowed to sit under a rabbi's teaching. What does this tell you about the lengths God will go to in pursuing a woman's heart?

What was the end result of Jesus's pursuit of this woman's heart?

Is this story about what Jesus wanted *from* this woman or what God wanted *for* this woman?

6. How does John 6:44 show that God always makes the first move?

7. What part do trials and difficulties play in God's pursuit of our hearts? Read Psalm 119:67–75 and Psalm 107:4–9, 10–16, 17–22, 23–32. (Note the four times the writer said, "Then they.")

8. Take time today to write how God pursued your heart and brought you to saving faith. Then make a list of ten ways that He has continued to pursue your heart and drawn you into an intimate relationship with Him. The fact that He drew you to this book and study could be one of them.

Lesson 3: Living in Sacred Union

I am constantly amazed that the God of all creation invites me to live in union with Him. As you feast on the following verses at a table set for two, pray that God will show you what it means to exist in sacred union with Him.

1. In the temple, a veil hung in front of the holy of holies to separate the high priests from the presence of God. Read Mark 15:38. What happed to the curtain in the temple when Jesus died, and who did it?

Aren't you glad Jesus made a way for you to enter into constant communion and union with God? Because of

Jesus's finished work on the cross, how can you enter God's presence? Read Hebrews 4:14–16 and 10:19–24.

2. What do the following verses teach you about union with Christ?

> Romans 8:11
>
> Colossians 2:6–7; 3:3
>
> 1 Corinthians 1:30
>
> 1 Corinthians 6:15–17
>
> 1 John 4:10

3. Read Ephesians chapters 1 and 2, and note everything you learn about being in Christ.

4. Read and record Galatians 2:20. How is that a beautiful picture of sacred union?

5. When a married couple say that they have grown apart, what they really mean is that they have grown dissimilar. How might this parallel what happens when we feel distant from God?

If you have grown "dissimilar" to God, what do you need to do?

Read Revelation 2:4–5. What did John write to the church at Ephesus?

As in any relationship, distance grows gradually. However, sometimes we can put our finger on a particular point in time and say, "There. That is where this all started." Look for and identify any decisions in your life that may have led to a sense of distance from God.

6. Read Romans 11:17–18. What is our relationship with Jesus to resemble?

7. How did Jesus pray for our union with Him as well as with other believers in John 17:10, 20–23?

Francis Schaeffer wrote in *The Mark of a Christian* that if we really love each other, the world is drawn to Christ. But if we don't, the world dismisses us as just another club.

What did Jesus say would be the outcome of Christians living in unity with Him and with other believers?

8. In closing, read and record our theme verse for this study: Acts 17:28. Did God reveal anything new to you this week about what that might look like in your life? If so, record those insights in your *Sudden Glory* journal.

Lesson 4: Joining God in Continual Conversation

I want to hear from God today, don't you? Let's take a fresh look at God's Word to see how we can expect Him to speak to us and how we can tune our hearts to hear.

1. Elijah needed to hear a fresh message from God. Read 1 Kings 19:9–13. Where was God's voice found and where was it not found?

Which requires the listener to pay closer attention: a whirlwind or a whisper?

What does that tell us about how we can prepare to hear God speak to our hearts?

2. What does God promise in Jeremiah 33:3?

3. Read Isaiah 48:1, 12, 16–19. What did God tell His people to do time and time again? Why did He want them to listen? Was it something He wanted *from* them or *for* them?

4. Read Isaiah 50:4. What did Isaiah expect each morning?

   If God awakens your heart to listen, what do you need to do to hear?

5. Describe the tone of a conversation between two business partners.

   Describe the tone of a conversation between two people in love.

   Which one more resembles the way you converse with God?

   Would you say that your conversations with God are more focused on requests to control your environment or more focused on personal communication that fosters intimate relationship? Explain your answer.

6. Read Proverbs 3:32. What does God share with the upright?

   The NASB translates 3:32 as "He is intimate with the upright." One commentary said, "You will be privy to the intimate counsels (secrets) of God who 'is intimate with the upright.'"[44] The word *intimate* means "private counsel." The Hebrew root word means "to be tight, firm, pressed together." It paints a picture of two heads together as in sharing a confidence. What picture comes to mind as you think about God taking you into His confidence?

7. Read Exodus 33:11. How did God speak to Moses?

   Read James 2:23. What did God call Abraham?

   Read John 15:15. What did Jesus call His disciples?

   Read John 15:13. What does Jesus call you?

8. Henry David Thoreau wrote: "The question is not what you look at, but what you see."[45] Many people can look at the same situation, but not everyone sees the same picture. Everyone can hear the same words, but not everyone hears the same message.

   Read John 14:25–26; 16:13–15; Matthew 16:15–17. Who opens our eyes and ears to understand God's intimate messages?

   Let's pray that God will open our eyes to see and ears to hear!

9. In *The Reflective Life,* Ken Gire wrote, "He comes to us in ways that require more than our eyes to see. He speaks to us in ways that require more than our ear to hear. He comes to us in ways that require the whole of us to respond, because it is to the whole of us that He makes His appeal."

   What does Matthew 22:37 tell you about how God wants you to commune and communicate with Him and how God wants to commune and communicate with you?

10. Record in your *Sudden Glory* journal what God has revealed to you in this lesson.

Lesson 5: Daring to Raise Your Expectations

Do you expect to experience God's presence and working in your life today? Do you expect to sense His presence and experience a

moment of sudden glory? In this lesson, we will see how God longs
for us to raise our expectations about the abundant life Jesus came
to give.

1. What is the difference between believing *in* God and believing
   God?

   Which would you say describes you?

   Is Romans 4:21 true in your life?

2. What do Genesis 15:6 and Romans 4:3 say about Abraham? The Greek word for "believed" is *pisteuo* and means
   to be firmly persuaded as to something to believe...with
   the idea of hope and certain expectation.[46] How should
   believing God raise our expectations?

3. Read Mark 9:14–27. Describe the scene.

   How did Jesus try to raise the father's expectations?
   (See verse 23.)

   What was the father's honest response? (See verse 24.)

   Did Jesus reprimand him or scold his honesty? No

   What did Jesus do for the father and the son?

   What does this tell you about the freedom you have to
   pray for a stronger faith? Will God get mad at you for
   asking Him to increase your faith?

4. Read and record Psalm 5:3. Would you say that David
   had high or low expectations?

5. What question did Jesus ask Martha in John 11:23–26?
   How was He attempting to raise her expectations?

6. Raising your expectations in your relationship with
   Jesus is distinctly different from increasing your expectation of entitlement. God does not owe you or

me anything, but He does promise us blessings. The
moment we feel a sense of entitlement, bitterness
takes root. By contrast, when we see God's gifts as
undeserved blessings, gratitude bubbles over. Read
2 Peter 1:3–4. What has God given us?

7. Let's look at a man who had very low expectations for life.
Read 2 Samuel 4:4. Who was Mephibosheth, and what
happened to him as a little boy?

Jump ahead to 2 Samuel 9:1–8. When David took over
as king, what did he want to do for Jonathan's relatives?
What was Mephibosheth's response to David's summons?

Let's stop and consider the amazing truth that God
has invited you to *live and move and have your being in
Him.* Has your response to His invitation to union and
communion ever resembled Mephibosheth's response to
King David?

In 2 Samuel 9:9–13 we see that David ignored
Mephibosheth's low expectations and simply told him
what he was going to do for him. What was it?

Mephibosheth lived in Lo Debar, meaning "pasture-
less land." My very unofficial translation is that he lived
"below the bar." Are you living below the bar of what the
King wants for you, or are you accepting His invitation
to eat at His table every day? Explain your answer.

His table is set and your name card is beautifully
placed. How will you respond?

8. Read and record Jesus's words in John 11:40. What feelings does that inspire for you?

9. How do the words of Psalm 5:3 encourage you to rise each morning with renewed expectations to experience God's presence in your life?

10. Are you expecting God to make His presence known to you today? If so, keep your eyes and ears open. Then record how you experienced God's presence in your *Sudden Glory* journal!

Lesson 6: Saying Yes to God's Divine Dance

I've got on my dancing shoes today. When we grab hold of God's hand and join Him in the divine dance of obedience, we find ourselves moving gracefully through life, connected yet following His lead. Take a deep breath! God has an incredible journey mapped out just for you!

1. Read and record Isaiah 48:17–18. Why did God want the people to obey Him?

   What would have been the end result?

   Is that something that God wants *from* you or *for* you?

2. One way God shows Himself mighty is by using ordinary men and women who depend on His strength to accomplish great feats. What do the following verses teach about that?

   Zechariah 4:6

   Acts 4:13 (one of my favorite verses)

   1 Corinthians 1:27

   2 Corinthians 4:7–11

3. I could camp on Jeremiah 1:5–8 for days. When does God say He knew Jeremiah?

   When did He set him apart for the work He planned for him to do?

Why did Jeremiah have no reason to be afraid?

How do these same verses apply to you as you *live and move and have your being* in Jesus?

4. Read Exodus 3:7–14 and note how many times God used the word *I* in this passage.

Who did God say had come down to rescue the Israelites? (See verse 8.)

What was He inviting Moses to do?

What was God's response (in verse 12) to Moses's argument (in verse 11)?

The next time you sense God calling you to take a step of obedience, no matter how small or how big, I want you to remember the words of Exodus 3:12: "I will be with you." What difference will that make in your response?

5. Let's look at two amazing verses to ponder: Luke 1:38 and 45. What did Mary say to Gabriel after his message about her part in God's redemptive plan?

What did Elizabeth say about Mary when she walked into her home a few days later?

Could someone say that about you today? Let me! Blessed are you, dear sister, who has believed that what the Lord has said to her will be accomplished!

6. Lest we get nervous about what God will call us to do, what do the following verses promise?

Isaiah 64:4

Psalm 57:2

We're simply called to show up and watch. But we must show up!

7. God's power always follows obedience. Read the following, and note when the glory moment took place.

Joshua 3:14–17. The Jordan River parted after...

Joshua 6:20–21. The walls of Jericho fell after...

Luke 5:4–7. Peter's net began to break after...

Luke 17:11–14. The lepers were healed after...

John 9:6–7. The blind man was healed after...

8. When we obey, it is God who does the work for us. Read Acts 2. Also see Acts 5:14; 11:24; 13:48. Who added the believers to their number?

Like those early believers, I want to be a part of whatever God is doing, don't you? How exciting that He lets us participate!

9. When God calls us to take a step of obedience, He usually doesn't lay out the entire trip. What did He tell Abraham in Genesis 12:1?

Suppose Abraham had waited until he had more information?

Are you waiting for more information before taking the first steps of obedience? Suppose God is waiting for you to take the first step before He shows you the second? What might you be missing out on by waiting for more information?

10. Read and record the following verses, inserting your name in place of *you* and *we*.

Jeremiah 29:11

Ephesians 2:10

11. Read Isaiah 30:21, and note what you can expect from living out Acts 17:28 in your life.

What will you do when you sense God's prompting to join Him in His work, to join Him on the dance floor of life? The music is playing. His hand is extended.

Lesson 7: Trusting God in Tough Times

Have you ever felt as if you've slipped away from God's presence? Has God seemed far away when times got tough? Today, let's refocus our eyes to see where God is during our trials, heartbreaks, and broken dreams.

1. Read Isaiah 43:1–7. What does God say about His presence when you go through difficult times?

   Describe a time when you passed through an emotional fire or river of difficulties. In light of Isaiah 43:1–7, where was God during that experience?

2. Read Daniel chapter 3. It is long, but it's just too good to leave anything out. Look back at verse 15. What did the king say would happen if Shadrach, Meshach, and Abednego did not bow to Nebuchadnezzar's idol?

   What was their response? (See verse 18.)

   When the three young men were thrown into the fiery furnace, who did the king see walking around with them? (See verse 25.)

   You can go ahead and shout now! How does this relate to Isaiah 43:1–7 in a literal way?

   How does this relate to you?

   What was the end result of the boys' fiery trial? Who was glorified? (See verse 28.)

3. What does God promise you in Hebrews 13:5 and Isaiah 54:10?

Do you believe that? If so, can you picture union with Jesus as you walk through the trials?

4. We can easily fall into the trap of thinking that God has forgotten us during difficult times. How do we see that in David's words of Psalm 77:1–9?

Now read the rest of the psalm. What did David do to remind himself of the faithfulness of God?

5. Read and record Isaiah 63:9. In one single elegant sentence, we learn how God feels when we are going through distressing times. What comes to mind as you read it?

6. In John 14:1 what did Jesus encourage the disciples to do during the trials He knew were coming their way?

7. How does truly trusting God change the way we view our difficult circumstances?

8. What do the following verses tell us about trials?

James 1:12

2 Corinthians 4:17

1 Peter 4:12

1 Peter 1:4–7

The Greek word translated "various" in the NASB translation of verse 6 is *poikilos* and means "variegated, diverse, manifold." Everybody's trial will look a little different.

In verse 7, we see that word *glory* again. The ultimate goal of our lives is to reflect what?

9. The Bible tells us that trials are one way God refines or purifies us. According to Malachi 3:1–3, what is the purpose of a refining metal?

   How is it refined, and what comes to the top so that the refiner can skim it off? What is the end product?

   With that in mind, what is the hoped-for end product of a difficult trial?

   The refiner knows the metal is purified when he can see his reflection in the liquid. How does that relate to the refining process in your life?

10. Perhaps one of the greatest glory moments of all is when we emerge on the other side of a tremendous struggle more alive to God's presence than ever before. Read Job 42:5. What did Job say at the end of his trials?

   Isn't that what we all want? I don't want to simply hear *about* God, I want to hear *from* God. I want to see His glory all around.

11. What did Paul say in Romans 8:18 about how our present sufferings will compare to the glory that is yet to come? That will be a sudden glory worth waiting for!

   I think many of the psalms are simply David's *Sudden Glory* journal entries. What do your own journal entries reveal? Take some time to read back over them or make a new entry today.

Lesson 8: Seeing God Through the Lens of Gratitude and Grace

Salvation does not ensure satisfaction. We can be saved from sin and still remain ungrateful, grumpy people. Quite often, ingratitude shields our eyes from recognizing moments of sudden glory. Let's spend this lesson looking at how gratitude and grace open our eyes and ears to sense God's presence.

1. What do you think is the best cure for ingratitude?

2. Read the following, and note the attitude of the Israelites, who woke up every day to a new and fresh miracle of God.

   > Exodus 15:24; 16:2; 17:3
   >
   > Numbers 14:29; 16:41
   >
   > Deuteronomy 1:27
   >
   > Psalm 106:25
   >
   > According to Numbers 11:1, how did God feel about their complaining?

3. What does Romans 1:21 say that the people did not do? What is that a sign of?

   > When we complain about life, who are we ultimately complaining about?

4. What does Philippians 4:6 tell you about how to pray?

   > What will be the result of such an attitude of prayer?
   >
   > This peace of mind is an inner tranquility that comes from knowing that God has everything under control. How does that certainty allow you to give thanks even as you pray in difficult situations?

5. Read Jehoshaphat's prayer in 2 Chronicles 20:5–12, 20–22. How did he sandwich his request in between two thick slices of praise and gratitude? (If you want to really be blessed, continue reading this chapter to see how God performed a miracle!)

6. How does ingratitude show a lack of trust?

    Read Habakkuk 3:17–19. What did Habakkuk say he was going to do, even though he didn't see the answers to all his prayers? Can you praise God with a grateful heart even if you do not see the answers to your prayers?

    Do you trust that He has everything under His control and has your best interests at heart? In what ways do your thoughts, words, and actions confirm your answer?

7. Why do you think praise is rooted in the trustworthiness of God, not in our circumstances?

8. Compare Philippians 2:14 and Colossians 3:17. How does complaining or grumbling show dissatisfaction with God?

    How is gratitude the opposite of complaining?

9. Let's take a moment to look at something we really need to be thankful for: God's grace. Look up and define *grace*.

    What do Romans 3:22–23 and Romans 8:1–2 tell you about God's grace?

10. Read Ephesians 1:6. How was God's grace given to us? What price did you pay? What price did Jesus pay?

11. Look up the following, and note the price Jesus paid so that you could live in union with Him.

    Romans 3:24
    Ephesians 1:7
    Colossians 1:14
    Hebrews 9:12–15

12. Read Galatians 5:1. Would you say you act more like a captive set free or a prisoner on parole? What is the difference?

13. End today's lesson by writing out a prayer of gratitude in your *Sudden Glory* journal.

Lesson 9: *Choosing Intimate Relationship over Routine Religion*

Today we're going to see what one family's story reveals about how much God longs to have a relationship with you. Regardless of what you've done or where you've been, He always waits for you with open arms.

1. Read Luke 15:1–3, 11–32. What request did the younger brother make?

    Did he care more about his relationship with his father or the things his father could give him?

2. The traditional Middle Eastern father would have thrown such a son out of the house empty-handed. What did this boy's father do? (See verse 12.)

    Describe what happened after the younger son spent his inheritance.

3. At what point did the son decide to humble himself and go home? (See verse 14.)

    What does this tell you about why God allows us to wallow in our own poor choices?

    Do you think it was painful for the father to let his son go out into the world, knowing what was going to happen to him?

    How do you think our heavenly Father feels when we do the same?

4. As the son approached home, where do we find the father? (See verse 20.)

   Can you visualize this father scanning the horizon day after day? Oh, how my heart swells at God's great love for us! How does this relate to what you learned in chapter 2 about God pursuing you?

5. Was the father more concerned with the restored relationship or the lost revenue from the squandered inheritance?

6. Now, put yourself at your heavenly Father's feet. When you come to Him, is He more concerned with your past mistakes or with the restored relationship? Explain your answer.

7. Did the father wait for the son to clean up his act and recite his repentance speech before he restored him into right relationship?

8. What did the son have to pay back to the father?

9. Now let's turn our attention to the elder brother, who is just as important to the story as the younger. What was his response to the father's forgiveness and willingness to restore the younger brother into right relationship? (See verse 28.)

   What did the elder brother's response reveal about how he valued his relationship with the father as compared to his father's possessions? (See verse 30.)

   Do you think that the elder, rule-keeping brother thought his father "owed him"? Explain your answer.

   Which brother was blind to his true condition?

   Which brother would have been quick to say he

needed a Savior? Which brother would have been quick to say he was doing pretty well on his own?

How does that relate to a person who is religiously legalistic rather than relationally living in union with Jesus?

10. Now let's go back to 15:1–3. Who was in the crowd listening to Jesus that day? Which group represented the younger son? Which group represented the older son?

We've traditionally read this parable as an example of how God welcomes home the repentant sinner, but suppose the real story was directed at the religious leaders who were listening. What was Jesus's message to them?

11. In Jesus's abrupt ending to the story, which brother was restored into right relationship and which brother was not? Keep in mind, the father reached out to both. He loved them both. He invited both to the party.

12. Jesus was reaching out to the very men who would eventually put him to death. How were Jesus's last words in this story of the prodigal son a plea for his worst enemies to get in right relationship with God?

13. You know what I have discovered? It is very easy to come to Jesus as the repentant younger brother and then gradually become the elder one. A sense of entitlement can creep in like hardening of the spiritual arteries. What can you do to keep yourself in a love relationship with Jesus and not become the pious, cold-hearted elder brother?

14. Luke 15:11–32 is called the parable of the prodigal son. But it is also a parable of the prodigal world. In summary,

how does this story illustrate God's desire to restore mankind, including you and me, into right relationship with Him?

Lesson 10: From Glory to Glory

God has placed eternity in our hearts, and we long to experience His glory right here on earth. While we only get glimpses during this thing called life, one day we will see Him face to face. In our final lesson, let's look at what lies in store for us.

1. Before we get into today's lesson, I want to revisit lesson 9. Review Luke 15:11–32. When the younger son asked for his inheritance, how was he saying that he wanted something more out of life?

   Did partying, possessions, people, and power satisfy his longing for something more? Explain your answer.

   Where did he finally go to find what he had been looking for?

   My hope is that each of us will "come to our senses" and realize that the only place the glory ache will ever be soothed is in the arms of our heavenly Father.

2. Read Revelation chapters 21 and 22, and record what you learn about your final home in glory.

   All through the book of Revelation, John used the word *like*. What does this tell you about our human ability or inability to describe God's glory?

3. Go back to chapter 1 in the book (not to be confused with lesson 1 in the study guide), and record what you learn about the word *glory*.

Why were you created? (See Isaiah 43:7.) Describe
what that means in your own words.

4. What do the following verses tell you about God's glory?

   Isaiah 6:3

   Psalm 19:1

   Psalm 97:6

   Psalm 138:5

5. Look in the dictionary for a definition of the word *display*.
   Read the following verses and note what you learn about
   Jesus being a display of God's glory.

   John 1:14

   John 2:11

   John 14:7–9

   Hebrews 1:3

6. What do the following verses say about how you are to
   display God's glory or splendor? (*Splendor* and *glory* are
   the same Hebrew word.)

   Isaiah 60:21

   Isaiah 61:3

   John 17:22, 24

   2 Peter 1:3

7. Based on what you have discovered in *A Sudden Glory*,
   particularly that glory is how God makes Himself recognizable to and through you, how does 1 Corinthians
   10:31 tell you to approach all you do?

8. Read and record 2 Corinthians 3:17–18. What does this
   tell you about our spiritual growth process? What happens
   as our relationship with Jesus deepens?

9. Think of all the television commercials about fighting
   the effects of aging. If you are in a group, it will be fun to
   share about the ones you can recall.

   What does Philippians 3:20–22 tell us about the body
   we will one day receive? I'm not sure what that will be
   like, but we can be sure it will be better than the one we
   have now!

10. Let's look at two bookends of the Bible. Record Genesis
    1:1 and Revelation 21:4. How does Revelation 21:4 point
    us to the hope that is to come?

    According to Colossians 3:4, what is the basis for that
    hope?

11. In the final words of the Bible, we see an invitation. God
    is always in pursuit of you. He is always inviting you to
    come. Read and record Revelation 22:17.

    Will you grab hold of His outstretched hand?

12. In closing, list five truths from *A Sudden Glory* you are now
    applying as *you live and move and have your being in Jesus.*

This may be the end of our study together, but it is only the beginning of our journey, filled with moments of sudden glory. I
would love to know your answer to this last discussion point and
to hear about your moments of sudden glory. I've set up a special
page on my website for that very purpose. Visit www.sharonjaynes
.com to share your story. Stop by often and share your glory moments. They might be just the story someone needs to help her
sense God's presence in her life. I'll see you there!

ACKNOWLEDGMENTS

God has used so many people to point me toward moments of sudden glory. Gwen Smith and Mary Southerland, my ministry partners at Girlfriends in God, have been two of God's sleuthing glory seekers who have opened my eyes and ears to His glory all around.

A special thanks to…

Bill Jensen, who gave me wonderful direction and pushed me to take a leap of faith.

Alice Crider and Liz Heaney, who helped me get off my galloping horse of random thoughts and stay the course of my central message.

Carie Freimuth, Laura Barker, Amy Haddock, Stuart McGuiggan, Lynette Kittle, Candis Pflueger, Tim Vanderkolk, and Christopher Sigfrids for using their special gifts and talents to help spread the message of *A Sudden Glory*.

The women who shared their stories of sudden glory: Alice Crider, Grainnie Owen, Diane Baker, and Pam Shattuck, and many more.

My husband, Steve, whom God uses daily to provide moments of sudden glory as we live and move and have our being in Christ hand in hand.

God, who lavishly responds to my ache for something more by giving me glimpses of glory here on earth…and will continue to do so until I leave this place and reach my final destination where the glory ache will be no more.

NOTES

1. Ann Voskamp, *One Thousand Gifts* (Grand Rapids, MI: Zondervan, 2011), 66.

2. "Survey Reveals the Life Christians Desire," Barna Group, July 21, 2008, www.barna.org/congregations-articles/29-survey-reveals-the-life-christians-desire.

3. Bob Gilliam, "Spiritual Journey Evaluation," T-Net International, www.tnetwork.com.

4. W. E. Vine, Merrill F. Unger, William White Jr., *Vine's Complete Expository Dictionary of Old and New Testament Words* (Nashville: Thomas Nelson, 1985), 267.

5. Sheldon Vanauken, *A Severe Mercy* (San Francisco: HarperSanFrancisco, 1980), 29.

6. James E. Bowley, *Living Traditions of the Bible: Scripture in Jewish, Christian, and Muslim Practice* (St. Louis, MO: Chalice Press, 1999), 192.

7. C. S. Lewis, *Mere Christianity* (Nashville: Simon & Shuster, 1980), 79.

8. A. W. Tozer, *The Pursuit of God* (Camp Hill, PA: Christian Publications, 2007), 20.

9. Tozer, *Pursuit of God*, 35.

10. Simon Tugwell, quoted in Brent Curtis and John Eldredge, *The Sacred Romance* (Nashville: Thomas Nelson, 1997), 69.

11. Vanauken, *Severe Mercy*, 25–26.

12. C. S. Lewis, *The Weight of Glory and Other Addresses* (Grand Rapids, MI: Eerdmans, 1965), 10.

13. K. D. Tessendorf, "White Knuckles of Niagara," Highlights Kids (September 1998), http://highlightskids.com/Stories/NonFiction /NF0998_niagaraKnuckles.asp. The author's account of Blondin's Niagara feats is drawn from this article.

14. *Spurgeon's Expository Encyclopedia: Sermons by Charles H. Spurgeon,* vol. 5 (Grand Rapids, MI: Baker Book House, 1998), 147.

15. Andrew Murray, *Abide in Christ* (Fort Washington, PA: Christian Literature Crusade, 1968, 1974), 12–13.

16. Brother Lawrence, *The Practice of the Presence of God,* trans. Robert J. Edmonson (Brewster, MA: Paraclete Press, 1985), 17.

17. Vanauken, *Severe Mercy,* 27.

18. C. S. Lewis, *Mere Christianity* (New York: Simon & Schuster, 1996), 169.

19. Warren W. Wiersbe, ed., *The Best of A. W. Tozer* (Camp Hill, PA: Christian Publications, 1980), 149.

20. Elizabeth Barrett Browning, "From 'Aurora Leigh,'" *The Oxford Book of English Mystical Verse,* D. H. S. Nicholson and A. H. E. Lee, eds., (Oxford: Claridon Press, 1917), www.bartleby.com /236/86.html.

21. Henry and Richard Blackaby, *Hearing God's Voice* (Nashville: Broadman & Holman, 2002), 140.

22. Voskamp, *One Thousand Gifts,* 107.

23. Annie Dillard, quoted in Curtis and Eldridge, *Sacred Romance,* 209.

24. Gene Weingarten, "Pearls Before Breakfast," *Washington Post* (April, 8, 2007), www.washingtonpost.com/wp-dyn/content /article/2007/04/04/AR2007040401721.html.

25. C. S. Lewis, *The Weight of Glory and Other Addresses* (New York: Harper Collins, 1976, 1980), 46.

26. Lewis, *Weight of Glory,* 26.

27. Brennan Manning, *The Furious Longing of God* (Colorado Springs: David C. Cook, 2009), 117.

28. Henry T. Blackaby and Richard Blackaby, *Experiencing God Day-by-Day* (Nashville: Broadman & Holman, 1997).

29. Attributed to Sir Francis Drake, a prayer penned as he was about to set sail in 1577, "Disturb Us, O Lord," Church Edge (November 1, 2007), http://churchedge.blogspot.com/2007/11/disturb-us-o-lord.html.

30. D. R. W. Wood and I. H. Marshall, *New Bible Dictionary,* 3rd ed. (Leicester, England; Downers Grove, IL.: InterVarsity, 1996), 358.

31. *Mounce's Complete Expository Dictionary of Old and New Testament Words,* (Grand Rapids, MI: Zondervan, 2006) 165–166.

32. Manning, *Furious Longing of God,* 77.

33. Rick Warren, *The Purpose Driven Life* (Grand Rapids, MI: Zondervan, 2002), 233.

34. Voskamp, *One Thousand Gifts,* 22.

35. Philip Yancey, *Disappointment with God* (Grand Rapids, MI: Zondervan, 1988), 90.

36. Jean-Pierre de Caussade, quoted in Rueben Job and Norman Shawchuck, eds., *A Guide to Prayer for All God's People* (Nashville: Upper Room, 1990), 244.

37. C. S. Lewis, *God in the Dock* (Grand Rapids, MI: Eerdmans, 1994), 52.

38. James Dobson, *When God Doesn't Make Sense* (Wheaton, IL: Tyndale House, 1993), 8.

39. Henry Ward Beecher, *Life Thoughts, Gathered from the Extemporaneous Discourses of Henry Ward Beecher* (New York: Sheldon, 1860), 115, http://books.google.combooks?id =0ukXAAAAYAAJ&printsec=frontcover&source=gbs_ge _summary_r&cad=0#v=onepage&q&f=false.

40. Jean Baptiste Massieu, quoted in Robert A. Emmons, *Thanks! How the New Science of Gratitude Can Make You Happier* (New York: Houghton Mifflin, 2007), 89.

41. Beth Moore, *Breaking Free* (Nashville: LifeWay Press, 1999), 170.

42. Wood and Marshall, *New Bible Dictionary,* 615.

43. *Mounce's Complete Expository Dictionary,* 613.

44. Jim Newheiser, *Opening Up Proverbs* (United Kingdom: Day One Publications, 2008), 68.

45. Edwin Way Teale, ed., *The Thoughts of Thoreau* (New York: Dodd, Mead, 1962), 231.

46. Vine, Unger, and White, *Complete Expository Dictionary,* 61.

ABOUT THE AUTHOR

Sharon Jaynes is an international conference speaker and the author of eighteen books, including *The Power of a Woman's Words, Becoming the Woman of His Dreams, Becoming a Woman Who Listens to God,* and *I'm Not Good Enough and Other Lies Women Tell Themselves.* Her books have been translated into several languages and continue to impact women for Christ all around the world.

Sharon is also the cofounder of Girlfriends in God, a nonde-nominational conference and online ministry that seeks to cross generational, racial, and denominational boundaries to bring the body of Christ together as believers. Their online devotions reach approximately five hundred thousand subscribers daily. To learn more visit www.GirlfriendsInGod.com.

Sharon and her husband, Steve, live in North Carolina and have one grown son, Steven.

Sharon is always honored to hear from her readers. You can e-mail her directly at Sharon@SharonJaynes.com or reach her by mail at:

Sharon Jaynes

PO Box 725

Matthews, North Carolina 28106

To learn more about Sharon's books and ministry, or to inquire about having Sharon speak at your next event, visit www.Sharon Jaynes.com.